D. G. Ristad

Lutheran Hymnal for the Sunday School

D. G. Ristad

Lutheran Hymnal for the Sunday School

ISBN/EAN: 9783337038533

Printed in Europe, USA, Canada, Australia, Japan

Cover: Foto ©Lupo / pixelio.de

More available books at **www.hansebooks.com**

LUTHERAN HYMNAL

FOR THE

SUNDAY SCHOOL.

಄ ಄ ಄ ಄ ಄

COMPILED BY

REV. D. G. RISTAD,

ROCKDALE, WIS.

಄ ಄ ಄ ಄

PRICE 25 CENTS.

಄ ಄ ಄ ಄

PUBLISHED BY

LUTHERAN SUNDAY SCHOOL PUBLISHING CO.,

734 W. NORTH AVE., CHICAGO, ILL.

SUGGESTIONS.

The *Superintendent* of the Sunday school should see that the following suggestions concerning the proper use of this Hymnal are heeded:

1. The *Organist* should learn to play these melodies correctly; that is, according to the music, giving due emphasis to the rhythm, which is the main characteristic of this little Hymnal as far as the melodies are concerned.

2. The *Teachers* also should endeavor to meet with the organist and learn to sing the melodies correctly, in order that they may be able to lead the singing in the Sunday school.

3. The *Children* should be taught to sing properly; that is, with a *natural voice* and in such manner that they say all the words in the text plainly and pronounce the syllables in every word distinctly; FOR THE MELODY IS THE SERVANT OF THE TEXT.

Opening Service.

1. Hymn.

2. One of the following Psalms shall be read responsively.

PSALM I.

BLESSED is the man that walketh not in the counsel of the ungodly: Nor standeth in the way of sinners, nor sitteth in the seat of the scornful.
But his delight is in the law of the Lord:
And in His law doth he meditate day and night.
And he shall be like a tree planted by the rivers of water:
That bringeth forth his fruit in his season.
His leaf also shall not wither:
And whatsoever he doeth shall prosper.
The ungodly are not so:
But are like the chaff which the wind driveth away.
Therefore the ungodly shall not stand in the judgment:
Nor sinners in the congregation of the righteous.
For the Lord knoweth the way of the righteous:
But the way of the ungodly shall perish.

PSALM XXIII.

THE Lord is my Shepherd:
I shall not want.
He maketh me to lie down in green pastures:
He leadeth me beside the still waters.

2

He restoreth my soul:
He leadeth me in the paths of righteousness for His Name's sake.
Yea, though I walk through the valley of the shadow of death, I will fear no evil:
For Thou art with me; Thy rod and Thy staff they comfort me.
Thou preparest a table before me in the presence of mine enemies:
Thou anointest my head with oil; my cup runneth over.
Surely goodness and mercy shall follow me all the days of my life:
And I will dwell in the house of the Lord for ever.

PSALM LXI.

Hear my cry, O God: attend unto my prayer.
From the end of the earth will I cry unto Thee, when my heart is overwhelmed:
Lead me to the Rock that is higher than I.
For Thou hast been a shelter for me: and a strong tower from the enemy.
I will abide in thy tabernacle forever: I will trust in the covert of Thy wings.
Selah.
For Thou, O God, hast heard my vows: Thou hast given me the heritage of those
that fear Thy name.
Thou wilt prolong the king's life:
And his years as many generations.
He shall abide before God forever:
O prepare mercy and truth, which may preserve him.
So will I sing praise unto Thy name forever: that I may daily perform my vows.

PSALM LXVII.

GOD BE merciful unto us and bless us:
And cause His face to shine up on us.
That Thy way may be known up on earth:
Thy saving health among all nations.
Let the people praise Thee, O God:
Let all the people praise Thee.
O let the nations be glad and sing for joy:
For Thou shalt judge the people righteously, and govern the nations upon earth.
Let the people praise Thee, O God:
Let all the people praise Thee.
Then shall the earth yield her increase:
And God, even our own God, shall bless us.
God shall bless us:
And all the ends of the earth shall fear Him.

PSALM LXXXV.

LORD, Thou hast been favorable unto Thy land:
Thou hast brought back the captivity of Jacob.
Thou hast forgiven the iniquity of Thy people:

Thou hast covered all their sin.

Thou hast taken away all Thy wrath:

Thou hast turned Thyself from the fierceness of Thine anger.

Turn us, O God of our salvation:

And cause Thine anger toward us to cease.

Wilt Thou be angry with us for ever?:

Wilt Thou draw out Thine anger to all generations?

Wilt Thou not revive us again:

That Thy people may rejoice in Thee?

Shew us Thy mercy, O Lord:

And grant us Thy salvation.

I will hear what God the Lord will speak:

For He will speak peace unto His people, and to His saints; but let them not turn again to folly.

Surely His salvation is nigh them that fear Him.

That glory may dwell in our land.

Mercy and truth are met together:

Righteousness and peace have kissed each other.

PSALM C.

MAKE a joyful noise unto the Lord, all ye lands:

Serve the Lord with gladness, come before His presence with singing.

Know ye that the Lord He is God:

It is He that hath made us, and not we ourselves; we are His people, and the sheep of His pasture.

Enter into His gates with thanksgiving, and into His courts with praise:

Be thankful unto Him, and bless His Name.

For the Lord is good; His mercy is everlasting:

And His truth endureth to all generations.

PSALM CI.

I will sing of mercy and judgment: unto Thee, O Lord, will I sing.

I will behave myself wisely in a perfect way: O when wilt Thou come unto me?

I will walk within my house with a perfect heart.

I will set no wicked thing before mine eyes:

I hate the work of them that turn aside; it shall not cleave to me.

A froward heart shall depart from me; I will not know a wicked person.

Whoso privily sundereth his neighbor, him will I cut off: him that hath an high look and a proud heart will not I suffer.

Mine eyes shall be upon the faithful of the land, that they may dwell with me: he that walketh in a perfect way, he shall serve me.

He that worketh deceit shall not dwell within my house: he that telleth lies shall not tarry in my sight.

I will early destroy all the wicked of the land:

That I may cut off all wicked doers from the City of the Lord.

PSALM CXI.

PRAISE ye the Lord. I will praise the Lord with my whole heart:
In the assembly of the upright, and in the congregation.
The works of the Lord are great:
Sought out of all them that have pleasure therein.
His work is honorable and glorious:
And His righteousness endureth for ever.
He hath made His wonderful works to be remembered:
The Lord is gracious and full of compassion.
He hath given meat unto them that fear Him:
He will ever be mindful of His covenant.
I will offer to Thee the sacrifice of thanksgiving:
And will call upon the Name of the Lord.
I will pay my vows unto the Lord now, in the presence of all His people:
In the courts of the Lord's house, in the midst of thee, O Jerusalem. Praise
ye the Lord.

3. The Apostolic Creed shall be said in concert.

4.   Gloria Patri.

THOMAS MORLEY.

Glo - ry be to the Fa-ther, and to the Son, and to the Ho - ly

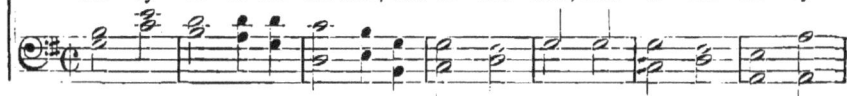

Ghost: As it was in the be - gin-ning, is now, and ev - er shall be,

world with-out end. A - - - - - men. A - men.

5

5. Prayer by Pastor; or, one of the following Collects may be said by the Leader of the Sunday School.

ENLIGHTEN our minds, we beseech Thee, O God, by the Spirit which proceedeth from Thee; that, as Thy Son hath promised, we may be led into all truth; through the same, our Lord Jesus Christ. Amen.

BLESSED Lord, Who hast caused all Holy Scriptures to be written for our learning: Grant that we may in such wise hear them, read, mark, learn, and inwardly digest them, that by patience and comfort of Thy holy Word, we may embrace, and ever hold fast the blessed hope of everlasting life, which Thou hast given us in our Saviour Jesus Christ. Amen.

ALMIGHTY God, our heavenly Father, whose mercies are new unto us every morning, and who, though we have in no wise deserved thy goodness, dost abundantly provide for all our wants of body and soul: give us, we pray thee, thy Holy Spirit, that we may heartily acknowledge thy merciful goodness toward us, give thanks for all thy benefits, and serve thee in willing obedience; through Jesus Christ thy Son, our Lord. Amen.

ALMIGHTY and Everlasting God, Who dost will that not one of these little ones should perish, and hast sent Thine Only Son to seek and to save that which was lost, and through Him hast said, Suffer the little children to come unto Me, and forbid them not; for of such is the kingdom of God. Most heartily we beseech Thee so to bless and govern the children of Thy Church, by Thy Holy Spirit, that we may grow in grace and in the knowledge of Thy Word; protect and defend us against all danger and harm, giving Thy holy Angels charge over us, through Jesus Christ our Lord. Amen.

6. Hymn.

7. Lessons.

Closing Service.

1. Hymn.

2. Announcements.

3. Review of day's Bible lesson; or, the Bible lesson for the following Sunday may be read and explained by the leader.

4. Hymn,

5. All shall unite in the Lord's Prayer.

LUTHERAN HYMNAL

FOR THE

SUNDAY SCHOOL.

---

1 ## Now Thank We All Our God.

MARTIN RINKART. 1644. JOHANN CRUGER. 1649.

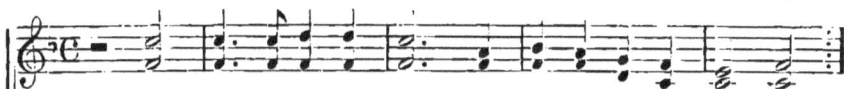

1. { Now thank we all our God, With hearts and hands and voic - es, }
{ Who wondrous things hath done, In whom His earth re - joic - es, }

2. { O may this bounteous God, Through all our life be near us, }
{ With ev - er joy - ful hearts, And bless-ed peace to cheer us, }

3. { All praise and thanks to God, The Fa-ther, now be giv - en, }
{ The Son and Him who reigns With them in high-est heav - en; }

Who from our mother's arms, Hath blessed us on our way
And keep us in His grace; And guide us when per-plexed,
The One e - ter-nal God, Whom earth and heav'n a - dore;

With count-less gifts of love, And still is ours to - day.
And free us from all ills, In this world and the next.
For thus it was, is now, And shall be ev - er - more!

7

2   All Glory be to God on High.

Nicholas Decius.   From Kyrie paschale by Schumann. 1539.

1. All glo-ry be to God on High, Who hath our race be-friend-ed!
2. We praise, we worship Thee, we trust, And give Thee thanks for-ev - er,
3. O Je-sus Christ, our God and Lord, Son of Thy Heavenly Fa - ther,
4. O Ho-ly Ghost, Thou precious Gift, Thou Com-fort-er un-fail - ing,

To us no harm shall now come nigh, The strife at last is end - ed;
O Father, that Thy rule is just, And wise, and chang-es nev - er;
O Thou who hast our peace re-stored And the lost sheep dost gath - er,
O'er Satan's snares our souls up-lift, And let Thy pow'r a - vail - ing,

God show-eth His good will to men, And peace shall
Thy bound-less power o'er all things reigns, Thou dost what-
Thou Lamb of God, to Thee on high, From out our
A - vert our woes and calm our dread: For us the

reign on earth a-gain; O thank Him for His good - ness.
e'er Thy will or-dains; Well for us that Thou rul - est!
depths we sin-ners cry, Have mer-cy on us Je - sus!
Sav-ior's blood was shed; We trust in Thee to save us!

8

3   Comfort, Comfort Ye My People.

JOHN OLEARIUS. (Oelschlæger.)   French. 42 Ps. 1551.

1. Com-fort, com-fort ye my peo-ple, Speak ye peace, thus saith our God;
2. For the Her-ald's voice is cry-ing In the des-ert far and near,
3. Make ye straight what long was crooked, Make the rough-er plac-es plain:

Com-fort those who sit in dark-ness, Mourning 'neath their sor-row's load;
Bid-ding all men to re-pent-ance, Since the king-dom now is here.
Let your heart be true and hum-ble, As be-fits His ho-ly reign;

Speak ye to Je-ru-sa-lem Of the peace that waits for them.
O that warn-ing cry o-bey! Now pre-pare 'for God a way!
For the glo-ry of the Lord Now o'er earth is shed a-broad,

Tell her that her sins I cov-er, And her war-fare now is o-ver.
Let the val-leys rise to meet Him, And the hills bow down to greet Him.
And all flesh shall see the to-ken, That His word is nev-er bro-ken.

9

4   Fear Not, O Little Flock.

MICHAEL ALLENBURG. 1640.   German. 1530.

1. Fear not O lit - tle flock, the foe   Who mad-ly seeks your
2. Be of good cheer; your cause be-longs   To Him who can a
3. As true as God's own Word is true,   Not earth or hell with
4. A - men, Lord Je - sus, grant our prayer!   Great Cap-tain, now Thine

o - ver-throw;   Dread not his rage   and pow - er,
venge your wrongs;   Leave it to Him,   our Lord.
all their crew   A - gainst us shall   pre - vail.
arm make bare,   Fight for us once   a - gain!

What tho' your cour - age some-times faints,   His seem-ing
Though hid - den yet   from mor - tal eyes,   His Gideon
A jest and by -   word are they grown;   God is with
So shall thy saints   and mar - tyrs raise   A might-y

tri - umph o'er God's saints, Lasts but a lit - tle hour.
shall for you a - rise,   Up-hold you and   His Word.
us; we are His own;   Our vic-t'ry can - not fail.
cho - rus to Thy praise,   World with-out end: A - men!

10

5   Lord, Jesus Christ.

H. C. STHEN, 16 Century. Tr. from Danish by
D. G. R. 1897.

L. M. LINDEMAN. 1871.

1. Lord Je - sus Christ, My Sav - ior blest, On Thee my hopes are found - ed. I trust in Thee, O leave not me In my mis - er - y In Thy word is my com - fort ground - ed.

2. And let Thy will To my heart in - still, That Thee I serve most tru - ly. Thou art my Lord, Teach me Thy word, And aye, a - ward More faith and pur - pose ho - ly.

3. In Thy do - main I will re - main, Dear Lord, where Thou wilt have me. My heart and mind Are on - ly Thine; In Thee I find Good gifts and grace to save me.

4. Most heart - i - ly I do be - lieve in Thy rich grace and fa - vor. Oh, Sav - ior sweet, Help me in need, For Thou didst bleed To save me from ev'ry ter - ror.

5 For evermore
Thou art therefore
My faith's source and foundation,
My solace sure,
For sin my cure;
Thy word so pure
Is my joy and salvation.

6 In grief's dread hour
Thou art my tower
Of strength and consolation.
I need not fear
When Thou art near;
Though foes appear,
I dread not their invasion.

7 In faith I rest,
Lord Jesus Christ,
Assured thou'lt ne'er forsake me,
For thus I read:
The Lord gives heed,
If in thy need
To prayer thou dost betake thee.

8 Grant God, we pray,
That we astray
From thy word wander never!
But that with Thee
Eternally
We blessed may be
In glory forever and ever.

6   Come Holy Spirit, God and Lord.

MARTIN LUTHER.

WALTER. 1524.

1. Come. Ho-ly Spir-it, God and Lord! Be all Thy grac-es now out-pour'd
2. Thou strong Defence, Thou ho-ly Light, Teach us to know our God a-right,
3. Thou sa-cred Ar-dor, Com-fort sweet, Help us to wait with read-y feet

On the be-liev-er's mind and soul, To strengthen, save, and make us whole
And call Him Fa-ther from the heart: The Word of life and truth im-part:
And will-ing heart at Thy com-mand, Nor tri-al fright us from Thy band

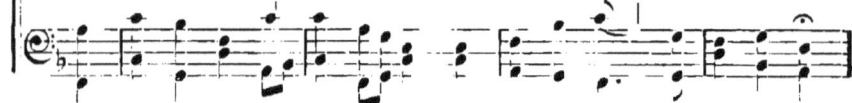

Lord, by the brightness of Thy light, Thou in the faith dost men u-nite
That we may love not doctrines strange, Nor e'er to oth-er teach-ers range,
Lord, make us read-y with Thy powers; Strengthen the flesh in weak-er hours,

Of ev-ery land and ev-ery tongue This to Thy praise, O
But Je-sus for our Mas-ter own, And put our trust, in
That as good war-riors we may force Through life and death to

Come Holy Spirit, God and Lord.

Lord, O	Lord, be sung.	Hal-le-lu -	jah, Hal-le-lu -	jah.
Him, in	Him a - lone.	Hal-le-lu -	jah, Hal-le-lu -	jah.
Thee, to	Thee our course!	Hal-le-lu -	jah, Hal-le-lu -	jah.

7 How Shall the Young Secure Their Hearts?

Isaac Watts. (1674-1748).　　　　　　　Nik. Herman. 1554

1. How shall the young se-cure their hearts And guard their lives from sin?
2. 'Tis like the sun, a heav'n-ly light, That guides us all the day;
3. The star-ry heav'ns Thy rule o - bey, The earth main-tains her place;

Thy Word the choic-est rules im - part, To keep the conscience
And through the dan - gers of the night, A lamp to lead our
And these Thy serv - ants, night and day, Thy skill and power ex -

clean;.................... To keep the con - science clean.
way;..................... A lamp to lead our way.
press;.................. Thy skill and power ex - press.

4 But still Thy Law and Gospel, Lord,
　Have lessons more divine;
　Not earth stands firmer than Thy Word
　‖: Nor stars so nobly shine. :‖

5 Thy Word is everlasting truth;
　How pure is every page!
　That holy Book shall guide our youth,
　‖: And well support our age. :‖

13

8   Praise to the Lord! Almighty King!

JOACHIM NEANDER. (1640–1680), 1679.   STRALSUNDER GESANGB. 1665.

1. Praise to the Lord! the Al-might-y, the King of cre - a - tion! O my soul,
2. Praise to the Lord! who o'er all things so wondrously reign - eth, Shelters thee
3. Praise to the Lord! who doth prosper thy work and de-fend thee; Sure-ly His
4. Praise to the Lord! Oh, let all that is in me a - dore Him! All that hath

praise Him, for He is thy health and sal - va - tion! All ye who hear,
un - der His wings, yes, so gen - tly sus - tain - eth; Hast thou not seen
good-ness and mer - cy here dai - ly at - tend thee. Pon - der a - new
life and breath, come now with praises be - fore Him! Let the A - men

Now to His temple draw near, join me in glad ad - o - ra - tion.
How thy de - sires e'er have been Granted in what He or - dain - eth?
What the Al-might-y can do, If with His love He be - friend thee!
Sound from His peo-ple a - gain: Glad-ly for aye we a - dore Him.

9   O That I Had a Thousand Voices!

J. MENZER.   FREYLIEGHAUSEN. 1704.

1. O that I had a thousand voices! A mouth to speak with thousand tongues!
2. O that my voce might high be sounding, Far as the wide-ly distant poles;
3. Lord, I will tiell while I am liv - ing, Thy goodness forth with ev-'ry breath;
4. O Father, deign Thou, I beseech Thee, To list-en to my earth-ly lays;

14

O That I Had a Thousand Voices.

My heart which in the Lord re-joic-es, Then would proclaim in grateful songs,
My blood run quick with rapture bounding, Long as its vi - tal current rolls,
And greet each morning with thanksgiving, Un - til my heart is still in death,
A nobler strain in heaven shall reach Thee, When I with angels hymn Thy praise,

To all, wher-ev - er I might be, What great things God hath done for me.
And ev - 'ry pulse thanks-giving raise, And ev - 'ry breath a hymn of praise.
Yea, when at last my lips grow cold, Thy praise shall in my sighs be told.
And learn amid their choirs to sing Loud hal - le - lu-jahs to my King.

10   Old Hundred.

Rev. WM. KETHE. 1561.   G. FRANC.' 1545.

1. All peo-ple that on earth do dwell. Sing to the Lord with cheer-ful voice;
2. Know that the Lord is God in - deed; With-out our aid He did us make:
3. O en - ter then His gates with praise, Approach with praise His courts un-to:
4. For why? the Lord our God is good, His mer - cy is for - ev - er sure;

Him serve with mirth, His praise forth tell, Come ye be - fore Him and re - joice.
We are His flock He doth us feed, And for His sheep He doth us take.
Praise, laud and bless His name al - ways, For it is seem - ly so to do.
His truth at all times firm - ly stood, And shall from age to age en - dure.

11   Doxology. L. M.

Praise God, from whom all blessings flow;
Praise Him, all creatures here below·
Praise Him above, ye heavenly host;
Praise Father, Son. and Holy Ghost.

12   A Mighty Fortress is Our God.

Original form acc. to JOH'S ZAHN.   MARTIN LUTHER. 1529.

1. { A might-y for-tress is   our God, A trust-y shield and weap - on,
   { He helps us free from ev - 'ry need, That hath us now o'er tak - en

2. { With might of ours can naught be done, Soon were our loss ef-fect - ed;
   { But for us fights the val - iant One Whom God Himself e - lect - ed.

The old   bit - ter   foe means us dead-ly woe: Deep guile and
Ask ye   Who is   this? Je - sus Christ it   is   Lord of Sab -

great might are his dread arms in fight, On earth is not his e - qual.
a - oth, There is no oth - er God, He holds the field for-ev - er.

3 Though devils all the world should fill,
All watching to devour us,
We tremble not, we fear no ill,
They cannot overpower us.
This world's prince may still
Scowl fierce as he will,
He can harm us none,
He's judged the deed is done,
One little word o'er throws him.

4 The word they still shall let remain,
Nor any thank have for it.
The Lord's with us upon the plain
With His good gifts and Spirit;
Take they then our life,
Goods, fame, child and wife,
When their worst is done,
They have nothing won:
The kingdom ours remaineth.

13   My Inmost Heart Now Raises.

Unknown. 1592.   NICOLAUS HERMANN. 1598.

1. { My in - most heart now rais - es, In this fair morn-ing hour
   { A song of thank-ful prais - es To Thine al - might-y power,

2. { For Thou from me hast ward - ed All per - ils of the night;
   { From ev - 'ry harm hast guard - ed My soul till morn-ing's light.

16

My Inmost Heart Now Raises.

O God up - on Thy throne! To hon - or and a - dore Thee,
Hum-bly to Thee I cry: O Sav - ior have com - pas - sion

I bring my praise be - fore Thee, Thro' Christ, Thine on - ly Son.
And par - don my trans-gres - sion; Have mer - cy Lord, most high.

3 God shall do my advising,
  Whose might with wisdom blends;
  May He bless rest and rising,
  My efforts, means and ends!
  To God, forever blessed,
  Will I with mine confide me,
  And suffer Him to guide me
  As seemeth to Him best.

4 Amen! I say, not fearing
  That God rejects my prayer;
  I doubt not He is hearing
  And granting me His care.
  So I put forth my hands,
  And look not long behind me,
  But ply the task assigned me
  By God, as He commands.

14 Lord, in Thy Kingdom There Shall be.

J. AOSTICE.   Danish acc. to SCHJORRING.

1. Lord, in Thy kingdom there shall be   No aliens from each oth - er,
2. When in Thy courts be - low we meet   To mourn our sin - ful liv - ing,
3. Make us to hear in each sweet word   Thy ho - ly Spir - it call - ing

But ev - en as He loves Him-self   Each saint shall love His broth er,
And with u - nit - ed hearts re - peat   Con-fes-sion creed, thanksgiv-ing:
To oneness with Thy Church and Thee, That heav'nly bond fore-stall-ing.

4 One Baptism and one faith have we,
  One Spirit sent to win us,
  One Lord, one Father, and one God,
  Above, and through and in us.

5 Never, by schism, or by sin,
  May we that union sever,
  Till all to perfect stature grown,
  Are one with Thee forever.

Wake, Awake!

PHILIP NICOLAI.   PHILIP NICOLAI. (1556-1608), 1599.

1. { Wake, a-wake, for night is fly - ing, The watchmen on the heights are crying:
   { Midnight hears the welcome voic - es,   And at the thrilling cry rejoic - es:

2. { Zi - on hears the watchmen sing-ing, And all her heart with joy is springing,
   { For her Lord comes down all glo - rious, The strong in grace, in truth victorious,

3. { Now let all the heavens adore Thee, And men and angels sing before Thee,
   { Of   one pearl each shining por - tal, Where we are with the choir im-mor-tal,

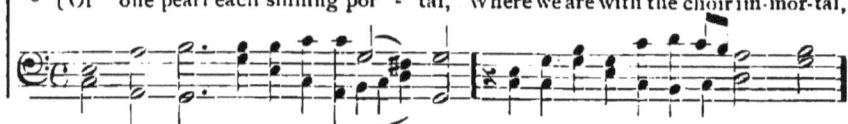

A-wake, Je - ru - sa - lem at last!)
Come forth, ye vir-gins, night is   ) past! The Bridegroom comes, awake,
She wakes, she ris - es from her gloom;)
Her Star is risen her Light is   ) come! Ah come, Thou blessed Lord,
With harp and cymbal's clear-est tone;)
Of   an-gels round Thy dazzling   ) throne; Nor eye hath seen nor ear

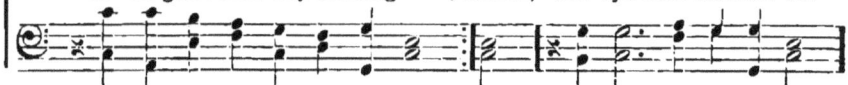

Your lamps with glad - ness take, Hal - le - lu - jah!
O   Je - sus, Son of God, Hal - le - lu - jah!
Hath yet at - tained to hear What there is ours,

And for His marriage feast pre-pare, For ye must go to meet Him there.
We fol - low till the halls we see Where Thou hast bid us sup with Thee,
But we re-joice, and sing to Thee Our hymns of joy e - ter - nal - ly.

16   From Greenland's Icy Mountains.

REGINALD HEBER. (1783–1819), 1826.   LOWELL MASON. (1792–1872), 1823.

1. From Green-land's i - cy moun - tains, From In - dia's cor-al strand,
2. What though the spic - y breez - es Blow soft o'er Cey-lon's isle;
3. Shall we, whose souls are light - ed With wis-dom from on high,
4. Waft, waft, ye winds, His sto - ry, And you, ye wa - ters, roll,

Where Af - ric's sun - ny foun - tains Roll down their gold - en sand;
Though ev - 'ry pros - pect pleas - es And on - ly man is vile:
Shall we to men be - night - ed The lamp of life de - ny?
Till, like a sea of glo - ry, It spreads from pole to pole;

From many an an - cient riv - er, From many a palm-y plain,
In vain with lav - ish kind - ness The gifts of God are strown:
Sal - va - tion, O sal - va - tion! The joy - ful sound pro - claim,
Till o'er our ran-somed na - ture The Lamb for sin - ners slain,

They call us to de - liv - er Their land from er - ror's chain.
The heath-en in his blind - ness, Bows down to wood and stone.
Till each re - mot - est na - tion Has learned Mes-si - ah's Name.
Re - deem-er, King Cre - a - tor, In bliss re - turns to reign.

19

17 Commit Whatever Grieves Thee.

PAUL GERHARDT. Died 1676.　　　　　HANS LEO HASLER. 1601.

1. { Com-mit what-ev - er grieves thee At heart, and all thy ways, }
   { To Him who nev - er leaves thee, On whom cre - a - tion stays. }
2. { The Lord thou must re - pose on If thou wouldst pros-per sure, }
   { His work must ev - er gaze on If thine is to en - dure. }

Who freest cours - es mak - eth For clouds, and air, and wind,
By anx - ious care and griev - ing, By self con-sum - ing pain,

And who care ev - er tak - eth A path for thee to find.
God is not moved to giv - ing; By prayer must thou ob - tain.

3 Though all the power of evil
  Should rise up to resist,
  Without a doubt of cavil
  God never will desist;
  His undertakings ever
  At length He carriest through;
  What He designs He never
  Can fail at all to do.

4 Hope on, thou heart, grief-riven,
  Hope, and courageous be,
  Where anguish thee had driven
  Thou shalt deliverance see.
  God, from thy pit of sadness
  Shall raise thee graciously;
  Wait and the sun of gladness
  Thine eyes shall early see.

18 Come, Holy Ghost.

B. RINGWALDT.　　　　　KLUG. 1535.

1. { Come Ho - ly Ghost, in faith us teach To love none but our Sav - ior, }
   { From all our heart, with all our might, And thus to serve Him ev - er; }
2. { Grant that Thy wholesome doctrine's pow'r May be our dear-est treas-ure, }
   { And let Thy word, the bread of life, Help us to heaven's pleas-ure. }
3. { When life and breath de-part from us In death's last aw-ful hour. }
   { Oh! may our hearts then re - al - ize The work-ing of Thy pow - er; }

Come, Holy Ghost.

That we 'gainst death, our fierc - est foe Find shel -
Yea, let us die to ev - 'ry sin, Re - vive
That we in - to our Sav - ior's hand With con -

ter in His wounds, and so Be res - cued by His mer - it.
the life of faith a - gain, To bear fruit of the Spir - it.
cious trust our souls commend, To gain rest ev - er - last - ing.

19 Jesus, Jesus, Jesus Only.

LUDAEMILIA ELIZABETH
of Schwarsburg, Roudolstadt.

L. M. LINDEMAN. 1871.

1. { Je - sus, Je - sus, Je - sus on - ly Can my heart-felt long-ing still; }
   { With-out Him my soul is lone-ly, And I wish, what Je - sus will. }

2. { One it is for whom I'm liv-ing, Whom I'm lov-ing faith-ful - ly; }
   { Je - sus, un - to whom I'm giv-ing What in love He gave to me. }

3. { Seems a thing to me a treas-ure, Which dis-pleas-ing is to Thee, }
   { Then remove such dangerous pleasure; Give instead what prof-its me. }

For my heart, which He hath filled, Ev - er cries: Lord, as Thou wilt.
Je - sus' blood hides all my guilt; Lord, O lead me as Thou wilt.
Let my heart by Thee be stilled, Make me Thine, Lord, as Thou wilt.

4 Grant that always I endeavor
   Thy good pleasure to fulfill,
In me, through me, with me ever,
   Lord, accomplish Thou Thy will.
Let me die, Lord, on Thee built,
When, and where, and as Thou wilt.

5 Lord, my praise shall be unceasing,
   For Thou gav'st Thyself to me,
And besides so many a blessing,
   That I sing now joyfully:
Be it unto me, my Shield,
   As Thou wilt, Lord, as Thou wilt.

20   Beautiful Savior!

From the German. 1695.   12th Century.

1. Beau - ti - ful Sav - ior! King of Cre - a - tion! Son of
2. Fair are the mead - ows, Fair - er the wood - lands, Robed in
3. Fair is the sun - shine, Fair - er the moon - light And the
4. Beau - ti - ful Sav - ior! Lord of the na - tions! Son of

God and Son of Man! Tru - ly I'd love Thee, Tru - ly I'd
flowers of bloom-ing Spring; Je - sus is fair - er, Je - sus is
spark-ling stars on high: Je - sus shines bright-er, Je - sus shines
God and Son of Man! Glo - ry and hon - or, Praise, ad - o -

serve Thee, Light of my soul, my Joy, my Crown.
pur - er; He makes our sorrow - ing spir - it sing.
pur - er, Than all the an - gels in the sky.
ra - tion, Now and for - ev - er - more be Thine.

21   O Morning Star!

PHILIP NICOLAI.   PHILIP NICOLAI (1556-1608), 1599.

1. { O Morning Star! how fair and bright! Thou beamest forth in truth and light!
   { Thou Root of Jes - se, David's Son, My Lord and Bridegroom, Thou hast won
2. { Thou heav'nly Brightness! Light Divine! O deep within my heart now shine,
   { Fill me with joy and strength to be Thy member, ever joined to Thee

O Morning Star.

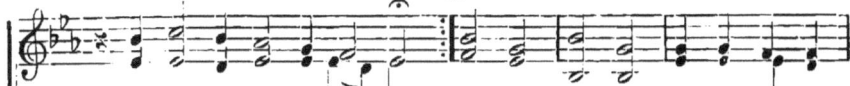

O Sov'reign meek and low - ly.
My heart to serve Thee sole - ly!
And make Thee there an al - tar!
In love that can-not fal - ter;

Ho - ly art Thou, Fair and gracious,
Toward Thee longing Doth pos-sess me,

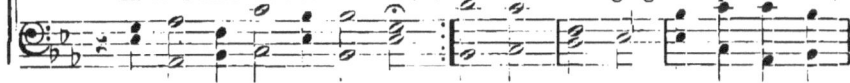

All vic -to-rious, Rich in blessing, Rule and might o'er all pos-sess - ing.
Turn and bless me, For Thy gladness Eye and heart here pine in sad - ness

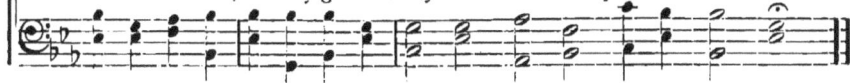

3 But if Thou look on me in love,
There straightway falls from God above
A ray of purest pleasure;
Thy Word and Spirit, Flesh and Blood,
Refresh my soul with heavenly food,
Thou art my hidden treasure;
Let Thy grace, Lord, warn and cheer me,
O draw near me;
Thou hast taught us
Thee to seek since Thou hast sought us!

4 Here will I rest, and hold it fast,
The Lord I love is First and Last,
The End as the Beginning!
Here I can calmly die, for Thou
Wilt raise me where Thou dwellest now,
Above all tears, all sinning:
Amen! Amen! Come, Lord Jesus,
Soon release us;
With deep yearning,
Lord, we look for Thy returning.

22 Lord Jesus Christ, Be Present Now.

WILLIAM II., Duke of Sax-Weimar. 1638.   Cant. Sac. Gotha 1648.

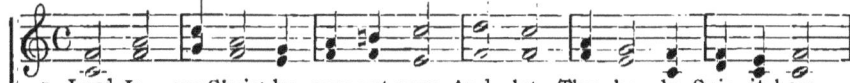

1. Lord Je - sus Christ be pres-ent now, And let Thy ho - ly Spir - it bow.
2. O - pen our lips to sing Thy praise, Our hearts in true de - vo-tion raise,
3. Un - til we join the host that cry: "Ho - ly art Thou, O Lord most high!"
4. Glo - ry to God, the Fa-ther, Son, And Ho - ly Spir - it, Three in One!

All hearts in love and fear to - day, To hear the truth and keep Thy way.
Strengthen our faith, increase our light, That we may know Thy name a-right:
And 'mid the light of that blest place Shall gaze up-on Thee face to face.
To Thee, O bless - ed Trin - i - ty, Be praise throughout e - ter - ni - ty!

23   Lord, Keep us Steadfast in Thy Word.

MARTIN LUTHER. (1483–1546), 1541.   MARTIN LUTHER, Wittenberg. 1542.

1. Lord, keep us stead-fast in Thy Word: Curb those who fain by craft or sword
2. Lord Je-sus Christ, Thy power make known; For Thou art Lord of lords a - lone:
3. O Com-fort - er, of price-less worth, Send peace and u - ni - ty on earth,

Would wrest the kingdom from Thy Son, And set at naught all He has done.
De - fend Thy Christendom, that we May ev - er-more sing praise to Thee.
Sup - port us in our fi - nal strife, And lead us out of death to life.

24

1 Lord Jesus Christ, with us abide;
While fall the shades of eventide;
Let not the radient light divine
Of Thy dear word e'er cease to shine.

2 In these sad latter days may we,
Vouchsafe this, Lord, e'er steadfast be.
And keep Thy word and sacrament
In purity unto the end.

3 Rebuke the spirits that, in pride
Exalting self, would set aside
Thy word, and bring devices new,
Corrupting, Lord, Thy doctrine true.

4 Not ours the cause is, but Thine own;
Not ours the glory, Thine alone;
Wherefore Thy people, Lord, defend,
Who trustingly in Thee depend.

5 Our heart's firm trust is e'er Thy word,
It is Thy Church's shield and sword:
O, keep us fast in this we pray,
That we may seek no other way.

6 Grant that according to Thy word
We here may live, and dying, Lord,
Still trusting in Thy word may we
Leave earth's sad vale to be with Thee.

                 N. SELNECKER.

25

1 Lord, grant that we e'er pure retain
The catechismal doctrine plain,
As Luther taught the heavenly truth
In simple words to tender youth.

2 That we Thy holy Law may know
And mourn our sin and all its woe,
And yet believe in Father, Son,
And Holy Spirit, Three in One.

3 That we on Thee, our Father, call
Who canst and wilt give help to all;
That as Thy children we may live,
Whom Thou in Baptism didst receive.

4 That, if we fall we rise again,
Repentingly confess our sin,
And take the sacrament in faith;—
Amen. God grant a happy death!

                 M. L. HELMBOLD.

26 From Heaven Above to Earth I Come.

MARTIN LUTHER.   MARTIN LUTHER.

1. From heav'n above to earth I come   To bear good news to   ev - 'ry home;
2. To you this night is born a child   Of Ma - ry, chos-en   vir - gin mild;
3. This is the Christ, our God and Lord, Who in all need shall aid af - ford;

Glad ti-dings of great joy I bring, Where-of I now will   say and sing.
This lit - tle Child of low-ly birth, Shall be the joy of   all the earth.
He will Himself your Sav-ior be, From all your sins to   make you free.

4 He brings those blessings, long ago
  Prepared by God for all below,
  That in His heavenly Kingdom blest
  You may with us forever rest.

5 Now let us all with gladness cheer,
  Follow the shepherds, and draw near,
  To see the wondrous gift of God,
  Who hath His own dear Son bestowed.

6 Give heed, my heart, lift up thine eyes!
  What is it in yon manger lies?
  Who is this Child so young and fair?
  Dear little Jesus lieth there.

7 Ah! dearest Jesus, holy Child,
  Make Thee a bed, soft, undefiled,
  Within my heart, that it may be
  A quiet chamber kept for Thee.

8 My heart for very joy doth leap,
  My lips no more can silence keep;
  I, too, must sing with joyful tongue
  That sweetest ancient cradle song:

9 Glory to God in highest heaven,
  Who unto man His Son hath given!
  While angels sing with pious mirth,
  A glad new year to all the earth.

27

1 The old year now hath passed away,
  We thank Thee Christ our Lord, to-day
  That Thou hast kept us through the year,
  When danger and distress were near,

2 We pray Thee, O Eternal Son,
  Who with the Father reign'st as one,
  To guard and rule Thy Christendom
  Through all the ages yet to come.

3 Take not Thy saving Word away,
  Our soul's true comfort, staff, and stay;
  Abide with us, and keep us free
  From all false doctrines graciously.

4 O help us to forsake all sin,
  A new and holier course begin:
  From last year's sins, Lord, hide Thy face,
  In this new year grant us Thy grace:

5 That as true Christians we may live,
  Or die in peace that Thou canst give,
  To rise again when Thou shalt come,
  And enter our eternal home.

6 There shall we thank Thee and adore,
  With all the angels evermore;
  Lord Jesus Christ, increase our faith
  To praise Thy name through life and death
                                    I. STEUERLEIN.

Joy to the World.

HANDEL.

1. Joy to the world, the Lord is come! Let earth re-ceive her King; Let
2. Joy to the world, the Sav-iour reigns; Let men their songs em-ploy; While
3. No more let sin and sor-row grow, Nor thorns in-fest the ground; He
4. He rules the world with truth and grace, And makes the na-tions prove The

ev - 'ry heart pre-pare Him room, And heav'n and nature sing; And
fields and floods, rocks, hills and plains. Re-peat the sound-ing joy; Re-
comes to make His bless-ing flow Far as the curse is found; Far
glo - ries of His right-eous-ness, And won-ders of His love; And

And heav'n and na-ture

Heav'n and na - ture sing,................. And heav'n and na - ture sing.
peat the sound-ing joy,................. Re - peat the sounding joy.
as the curse is found, ... Far as the curse is found.
won - ders of His love,................. And won - ders of His love.

sing. And heav'n and nature sing.

29 **Make Noises of Joy.**

Hundredth Psalm. D. G. R. 1897.   ERIK HOFF. About 1870.

1. Make nois - es of joy un - to the Lord ev - 'ry land!
2. Know ye that the Lord is God Je - ho - vah of old.
3. Thanks-giv - ing ye en - ter in - to His ho - ly gates!
4. The Lord He is good, and His mer - cy lasts al - way,

Make Noises of Joy.

Glo - ry be to God! With sing - ing come nigh and be-fore His pres-ence
Glo - ry be to God! He made us, not we our-selves, the lambs of His
Glo - ry be to God! His courts fill with praise, and His name declare and
Glo - ry be to God! His truth shall en - dure tho' the world may pass a -

stand! Re - joice in the Lord, ye His peo - ple!
fold. Re - joice in the Lord, ye His peo - ple!
bless! Re - joice in the Lord, ye His peo - ple!
way, Re - joice in the Lord, ye His peo - ple!

30 Help, Helper, help in Fear and Need.

JOH. JAK. LANG.   French. 1540.

1. Help, Helper, help in fear and need, Have mercy, to my pray'r give heed!
2. My God and Lord, I trust in Thee! What need I if Thou art with me?
3. Therefore my hap-pi - ness is great, I am content for Thee I wait,

I know Thou lov'st me still as Thine, Tho' 'gainst me world and hell combine.
And Thou, Lord Jesus Christ, art mine; My God and Sav-ior, I am Thine.
Trust wholly in Thy name, and then I pray: Help, Helper, help! A - men.

27

31 All Hail the Power.

Rev. E. Perronet. 1780.   O. Holden. 1793.

1. All hail the power of Je-sus' name! Let an-gels pros-trate fall;
2. Let ev-ery kin-dred, ev-ery tribe, On this ter-res-trial ball,
3. Oh, that with yon-der sa-cred throng We at His feet may fall;

Bring forth the roy-al di-a-dem, And crown Him Lord of all;
To Him all maj-es-ty as-cribe, And crown Him Lord of all;
We'll join the ev-er-last-ing song, And crown Him Lord of all;

Bring forth the roy-al di-a-dem, And crown Him Lord of all.
To Him all maj-es-ty as-cribe, And crown Him Lord of all.
We'll join the ev-er-last-ing song, And crown Him Lord of all.

32 Come, See the Place Where Jesus Lay.

Thomas Kelly. 1769-1855.   W. Stokes.

1. Come, see the place where Je-sus lay, And hear an-gel-ic watchers say,—
2. O joy-ful sound! O glorious hour, When by His own Al-might-y power,
3. The first be-got-ten of the dead, For us He rose, our glorious Head,
4. No more they trem-ble at the grave, For Je-sus will their spir-its save,

Come, See the Place Where Jesus Lay.

"He lives, who once was slain: Why seek the liv - ing 'midst the dead?
He rose and left the grave: Now let our songs His tri-umph tell,
Im - mor - tal life to bring: What tho' the saints like Him shall die,
And raise their slumb'ring dust: O Ris - en Lord, in Thee, we live,

Re - mem-ber how the Sav - ior said That He would rise a - gain."
Who burst the bands of death and hell, And ev - er lives to save.
They share their Lead-er's Vic - to - ry And tri - umph with their King.
To Thee our ransomed souls we give, To Thee our bod - ies trust.

33 Rock of Ages.

Rev. A. M. TOPLADY. 1776.   Dr. THOS. HASTINGS. 1830.

FINE.

1. Rock of A - ges, cleft for me, Let me hide my - self in Thee;
D. C.—Be of sin the dou - ble cure, Save me from its guilt and power.
2. Not the la - bor of my hands Can ful - fill Thy law's de-mands;
D. C.—All for sin could not a - tone; Thou must save and Thou a - lone.

D. C.

Let the wa - ter and the blood, From Thy riv - en side which flow'd,
Could my zeal no res - pite know, Could my tears for - ev - er flow,

3 Nothing in my hand I bring,
Simply to Thy cross I cling;
Naked, come to Thee for dress,
Helpless. look to Thee for grace;
Foul. I to the fountain fly,
Wash me, Savior, or I die.

4 While I draw this fleeting breath,
When mine eyes shall close in death,
When I soar to worlds unknown,
See Thee on Thy judgment throne,
Rock of Ages, cleft for me,
Let me hide myself in Thee.

29

34   Holy, Lord God Almighty.

R. HEBER, D. D.

REV. JOHN B. DYKES.

1. Ho - ly, Ho - ly, Ho - ly! Lord, God Al-might - y! Ear - ly in the
2. Ho - ly, Ho - ly, Ho - ly! all the saints a - dore Thee, Casting down their
3. Ho - ly, Ho - ly, Ho - ly! tho' the darkness hide Thee, Tho' the eye of

morn - ing our songs shall rise to Thee; Ho - ly, Ho - ly, Ho - ly!
golden crowns a-round the glas - sy sea; Cher - u - bim and Sera-phim
sin-ful man Thy glo - ry may not see, On - ly Thou art Ho - ly,

Mer - ci - ful and Might - y! God, whose dear presence fills e - ter - ni - ty.
fall - ing down be-fore Thee, Which wert and art, and ev - er-more shalt be.
there is none be - side Thee, Per - fect in pow'r, in love, and pur-i - ty.

35   Come, Thou Almighty King.

CHARLES WESLEY.

FELICE GIARDINI.

1. Come, Thou Al - might - y King, Help us Thy name to sing,
2. Come, thou in - car - nate Word, Gird on thy might - y sword;
3. Come, ho - ly Com - fort - er! Thy sa - cred wit - ness bear,
4. To Thee, great One in Three, E - ter - nal prais - es be

Come, Thou Almighty King.

Help us to praise: Fa - ther all glo - ri - ous, O'er all vic -
Our pray'r at - tend: Come, and Thy peo - ple bless, And give Thy
In this glad hour; Thou, who al - might - y art, Now rule in
Hence ev - er - more! Thy sovereign maj - es - ty May we in

to - ri - ous. Come, and reign o - ver us An - cient of Days.
word suc-cess; Spir - it of ho - li - ness! On us de - scend.
ev - 'ry heart, And ne'er from us de - part, Spir - it of pow'r.
glo - ry see. And to e - ter - ni - ty Love and a - dore.

36   Just as I Am.

MISS CHARLOTTE ELLIOTT. 1834.   WM. B. BRADBURY.

1. Just as I am, with - out one plea, But that Thy blood was shed for me,
2. Just as I am, and wait-ing not To rid my soul of one dark blot,
3. Just as I am, tho' tossed a-bout, With many a con-flict, many a doubt,

And that Thou bidd'st me come to Thee, O Lamb of God! I come, I come!
To Thee, whose blood can cleanse each spot. O Lamb of God! I come, I come!
Fight-ings and fears with-in, with-out, O Lamb of God! I come, I come!

4 Just as I am, poor, wretched, blind,
Sight, riches, healing of the mind,
Yea, all I need, in Thee to find,
O Lamb of God, I come, I come.

5 Just as I am, Thou wilt receive,
Wilt welcome, pardon, cleanse, relieve,
Because Thy promise I believe,
O Lamb of God, I come, I come.

37. Now God Be with Us.

P. HERBERT.
JOHAN CRUGER. 1640.

1. Now God be with us for the night is clos-ing; The light and
2. Let e-vil thoughts and spir-its flee be-fore us; Till morn-ing
3. Let pi-ous thoughts be ours when sleep o'er-takes us, Our ear-liest
4. Thro' Thy Be-lov-ed soothe the sick and weep-ing, And bid the

dark-ness are of His dis-pos-ing, And 'neath His
com-eth, watch, O Mas-ter, o'er us; In soul and
thoughts be Thine when morn-ing wakes us; All day serve
cap-tive lose his griefs in sleep-ing; Wid-ows and

shad-ow here to rest we yield us, For He will shield us.
bod-y Thou from harm de-fend us, Thine an-gels send us.
Thee, in all that we are do-ing, Thy praise pur-su-ing.
or-phans, we to Thee commend them, Do Thou de-fend them.

5 We have no refuge, none on earth to aid us,
Save Thee, O Father, who Thine own hast made us;
But Thy dear presence will not leave them [lonely
Who seek Thee only.

6 Father, Thy name be praised, Thy king-dom given,
Thy will be done on earth as 'tis in heav-en,
Give daily bread, forgive our sins, deliver
Us now and ever.

38 Now Rest Beneath Night's Shadows.

HENRI ISAAK.
HENRI ISAAK. 1536.

1. Now rest beneath night's shadows, Man, beast, town, woods and meadows, The
2. Lord, Je-sus, who dost love me, O spread Thy wings a-bove me, And
3. My loved ones rest se-cure-ly,—From ev-'ry per-il sure-ly Our

Now Rest Beneath Night's Shadows.

world in slum-ber lies; But Thou my heart a - wake Thee, To
shield me from a - larm! Though Sa - tan would de - vour me, Let
God will guard your heads. May He sweet slum - bers send you, And

pray'r and song be - take Thee, Let praise to thy Cre - a - tor rise.
an-gel-guards sing o'er me: "This child of God shall meet no harm."
bid His hosts at - tend you, And gold - en - armed watch o'er your beds.

39　　　　O, Jesus King.

BERNARD of Clairvaux (1091-1153).　　　　　G. F. HANDEL.

1. O Je - sus! King most won - der - ful, Thou con - quer - or re-nowned;
2. When once Thou vis - it - est the heart, Then truth be - gins to shine:
3. O Je - sus, Light of all be - low! Thou Fount of life and fire!

Thou sweet-ness most in - eff - a - ble, In whom all joys are found.
Then earth - ly van - i - ties de - part, Then kin - dles love di - vine.
Sur - pass - ing all the joys we know, All that we can de - sire.

4 May every heart confess Thy Name,
　And ever Thee adore;
And, seeking Thee, itself inflame
　To seek Thee more and more.

5 Thee may our tongues forever bless;
　Thee may we love alone;
And ever in our lives express
　The image of Thine own. Amen.

33

40 God Who Madest Earth and Heaven.

HEINRICH ALBERT.   HEINRICH ALBERT. 1642.

1. God who mad-est earth and heav-en, Fa-ther, Son, and Ho-ly Ghost,
2. Let the night of my transgression With night's darkness pass a-way:
3. Let my life and con-ver-sa-tion Be di-rect-ed by Thy Word;

Who the day and night hast giv-en, Sun and moon and star-ry host,
Je-sus, in-to Thy pos-sess-ion I re-sign my-self to-day.
Lord, Thy con-stant pres-er-va-tion To Thy err-ing child af-ford.

Thou whose mighty hand sus-tains Earth and all that she con-tains.
In Thy wounds I find re-lief From my great-est sin and grief.
No-where but a-lone in Thee From all harm can I be free.

4 Wholly to Thy blest protection
I commit my heart and mind.
Mighty God! to Thy direction
Wholly may I be resigned,
Lord, my Shield, my Light divine,
O accept and own me Thine!

5 Lord, to me Thine angel sending,
Keep me from the subtle foe;
From his craft and might defending,
Never let Thy wanderer go,
Till my final rest be come,
And Thine angel bear me home.

41 Abide With Me!

HENRY F. LYTE.   W. H. MONK.

1. A-bide with me! Fast falls the e-ven-tide; The dark-ness
2. Swift to its close ebbs out life's lit-tle day; Earth's joys grow
3. I need Thy pres-ence ev-'ry pass-ing hour, What but Thy
4. Not a brief glance I long, a pass-ing word; But as Thou

34

Abide With Me.

deep - ens— Lord, with me a - bide! When oth - er help - ers
dim, its glo - ries pass a - way; Change and de - cay in
grace can foil the temp-ter's pow'r? Who like Thy-self, my
dwell'st with Thy dis - ci - ples, Lord, Fa - mil - iar, con - de -

fail and comforts flee, Help of the helpless, oh, a - bide with me!
all a-round I see; O Thou who changest not, a - bide with me!
guide and stay can be? Thro' cloud and sunshine,oh. a - bide with me!
send - ing, pa-tient, free, Come, not to so-journ, but a - bide with me!

42 The Swift Declining Day.

H. G. NAGELL.

1. The swift de - clin - ing day, How fast it's mo - ments fly!
2. Ye mor - tals, mark its pace, And use the hours of light;
3. Give glo - ry to the Lord, Who rules the whirl-ing sphere;
4. Then shall new , lus - tre break Thro' death's im - pend-ing gloom,

While eve-ning's broad and gloom-y shade Gains on the west-ern sky.
And know its Mak - er can com - mand At once e - ter - nal night.
Sub - mis - sive at His foot-stool bow. And seek sal - va - tion there.
And lead you to un - chang-ing light, In your ce - les - tial home.

43 Lift Up Your Heads, Ye Mighty Gates.

GEORGE WEISSEL.   J. STOBÆUS.

1. Lift up your heads, ye might-y gates! Be - hold the King of glo - ry waits;
2. The Lord is just, a Help-er tried, Mer - cy is ev - er at His side;
3. O blest the land, the cit - y blest, Where Christ the Rul-er is con - fest!

The King of kings is drawing near, The Sav - ior of the world is here;
His king-ly crown is ho - li- ness, His scep-ter, pit - y in dis-tress,
O hap-py hearts and hap-py homes To whom this King in triumph comes!

Life and sal - va - tion He doth bring, Wherefore re - joice and glad-ly sing:
The end of all our woe He brings; Wherefore the earth is glad and sings:
The cloud-less Sun of joy He is, Who bring-eth pure de-light and bliss:

We praise Thee, Fa - ther, now, Cre - a - tor, wise art Thou!
We praise Thee, Sav - ior, now, Cre - a - tor, wise art Thou!
O Com - fort - er Di - vine, What bound - less grace is Thine!

4 Fling wide the portals of your heart;
Make it a temple, set apart
From earthly use for heaven's employ,
Adorned with prayer, and love. and joy;
So shall your Sovereign enter in,
And new and nobler life begin:
    To Thee, O God, be praise,
    For word and deed and grace!

5 Redeemer, come! I open wide
My heart to Thee; here, Lord, abide!
Let me Thy inner presence feel,
Thy grace and love in me reveal;
Thy Holy Spirit guide us on,
Until our glorious goal be won!
    Eternal praise and fame
    We offer to Thy name.

44 Come, Sing Our Christmas Lay!

(In Dulci Jubilo.)

From German 1646. Tr. by D. G. R. 1897.   14th Century.

1. Come, sing our Christmas lay, ... Re-joice, re-joice and say: ....
2. Oh, Son of God on high! .... I yearn to come Thee nigh! .... Be
3. Great is the Fa-ther's grace: ...... His Son takes sin-ner's place! I
4. Where is this joy - ful land? ...... It's where the hap-py band .... Of

In a man - ger low - ly   Lies our hearts' de - light ....
Thou my con - so - la - tion And my heart's com - fort here .... •
was in con-demn - na - tion Thro' sin and van - i - ty, ...
saints and an - gels' voic - es With psalms and mu - sic sweet ....

A Babe, sweet, pure and ho - - ly Ra-diant, fair and bright,   My
Be Thou my soul's sal - va - tion My hap - pi - ness and cheer!
But Christ by His sal - va - tion Gained heaven's joy for me,
Be-fore God's throne re - joic - es A - dor - ing at His feet,

on - ly joy is He; .... My on - ly joy is He.
Draw me un - to Thee; .... Draw me un - to Thee.
O that I were there! .... O that I were there!
O that we were there! .... O that we were there!

37

45 Great God, What Do I See and Hear.

Partly by WILLIAM B. COLLYER. MELCHIOR FRANCK. 1631.

1. { Great God, what do I see and hear! The end of things cre - at - ed! }
   { The Judge of man I see ap-pear, On clouds of glo - ry seat - ed. }
2. { The dead in Christ shall first a - rise, At the last trum - pet's sounding, }
   { Caught up to meet Him in the skies, With joy their Lord sur - round-ing; }

The trum-pet sounds: the graves re-store The dead which they con-
No gloom-y fears their souls dismay; His presence sheds e -

tained be - fore; Pre - pare, my soul, to meet Him.
ter - nal day On those pre - pared to meet Him.

3 But sinners, filled with guilty fears,
　Behold His wrath prevailing;
For they shall rise and find their tears
　And sighs are unavailing;
The day of grace is past and gone;
Trembling they stand before the throne,
　All unprepared to meet Him.

4 O Christ, who diedst and yet dost live,
　To me impart Thy merit;
My pardon seal, my sins forgive,
　And cleanse me by Thy Spirit.
Beneath Thy cross I view the day
When heaven and earth shall pass away,
　And thus prepare to meet Thee.

46　My Faith Looks Up to Thee.

RAY PALMER. LOWELL MASON.

1. My faith looks up to Thee, Thou Lamb of Cal - va - ry,
2. May Thy rich grace im-part Strength to my faint - ing heart,
3. While life's dark maze I tread, And griefs a - round me spread,
4. When ends life's tran - sient dream, When death's cold sul - len stream

My Faith Looks Up To Thee.

Sav - ior di - vine! Now hear me while I pray, Take all my
My zeal in - spire; As Thou hast died for me, Oh, may my
Be Thou my guide; Bid dark-ness turn to day, Wipe sor-row's
Shall o'er me roll; Blest Sav - ior! then, in love, Fear and dis-

guilt a - way, Oh, let me from this day Be whol - ly Thine!
love to Thee Pure, warm and changeless be, A liv - ing fire!
tears a - way, Nor let me ev - er stray From Thee a - side.
trust re-move; Oh, bear me safe a-bove, A ran - somed soul!

47   Emmanuel! We Sing Thy Praise.

PAUL GERHARDT (1606-1676), 1653. From LUDWIG VAN BEETHOVEN. (1770-1827).

1. Em-man-u - el! We sing Thy praise, Thou Prince of Life! Thou Fount of Grace!
2. E'er since the world be-gan to be, How many a heart hath longed for Thee!
3. Now art Thou here: we know Thee now; In low-ly man - ger li - est Thou;
4. Now fear-less I can look on Thee: From sin and grief Thou set'st me free:

With all Thy saints, Thee Lord, we sing; Praise. honor, thanks to Thee we bring.
And Thou, O long ex-pect-ed Guest, Hast come at last to make us blest!
A Child. yet mak-est all things great; Poor, yet is earth Thy robe of state.
Thou bearest wrath, Thou conquerest death, Fear turns to joy Thy glance beneath.

5 Thou art my Head, my Lord divine:
I am Thy member, wholly Thine;
And in Thy Spirit's strength would still
Serve Thee according to Thy will.

6 Thus will I sing Thy praises here,
With joyful spirit year by year:
And they shall sound before Thy throne,
Where time nor number more is known.

39

48   Nearer, My God, to Thee.

SARAH F. ADAMS.   LOWELL MASON.

1. Near-er, my God, to Thee, Near - er to Thee! E'en tho' it be a cross
2. Tho' like the wan-der-er, The sun gone down, Dark - ness be o - ver me,
3. There let the way ap-pear, Steps un - to heav'n; All that Thou sendest me,
4. Then with my waking tho'ts Bright with Thy praise, Out of my storm-y griefs

That rais - eth me!   Still all my song shall be, Near - er, my
My rest a stone.   Yet in my dreams I'd be Near - er, my
In mer - cy given;   An - gels to beck - on me Near - er, my
Beth - el I'll raise;   So by my woes to be Near - er, my

God, to Thee, Near - er, my God, to Thee, Near - er to Thee.
God, to Thee, Near - er, my God, to Thee, Near - er to Thee.
God, to Thee, Near - er, my God, to Thee, Near - er to Thee.
God, to Thee, Near - er, my God, to Thee, Near - er to Thee.

49

1 Nearer, my God, to Thee,
   Nearer to Thee!
E'en though it be a cross
   That raiseth me!
Still all my song shall be,
Nearer, my God, to Thee,
   Nearer, my God, to Thee,
     Nearer to Thee.

2 Nearer, my Lord, to Thee,
   Nearer to Thee,
Who to Thy cross didst come
   Dying for me!
Strengthen my willing feet!
Hold me in service sweet
   Nearer, O Christ, to Thee,
     Nearer to Thee!

3 Nearer, O Comforter,
   Nearer to Thee!
Who with my loving Lord
   Dwellest with me!
Grant me Thy fellowship!
Help me each day to keep
   Nearer, my Guide, to Thee,
     Nearer to Thee!

4 But to be nearer still,
   Bring me, O God!
Not by the visioned steeps
   Angels have trod.
Here where Thy cross I See
Jesus, I wait for Thee,
   Then evermore to be
     Nearer to Thee!

H. D. GANSE.

50   Set Bounds to Your Sorrow.

Prudentius. 405.   Wittenberg. 1542.

1. Set bounds to your sor - row and griev - ing,   And   seek   in God's
2. Bound up   in   its shroud, a-midst weep - ing,   This   corpse   is laid
3. Al - though now the heart   no more beat - eth   The   eye with thine

word   thy re - liev - ing;   Let   mourn - ing not grow   in - to
down   to its sleep - ing,   Let   em - blems of sleep   be the
own   nev - er meet - eth,   God's sleep - ing ones are   not for -

sin - ning;   This   dy - ing   is   true life's be - gin - ning.
to - ken,   That   one   day, death's bonds shall be bro - ken.
sak - en;   From   slum - ber He'll bid them a - wak - en.

4 This body, so waisted and shattered,
This dust that 'midst dust shall be scattered
Shall then be raised up, and inherit
New life with the glorified spirits.

5 The grain sown to-day in the furrow,
No trace leaves behind it to-morrow,
Yet lo, soon the fresh blade is springing,
Glad cheer to the husbandman bringing!

6 O Earth, we lay down in thy bosom
A seed from which life once shall blossom;
Receive it in charge of its Maker:
'Tis therefore we call thee God's acre.

7 A soul in this frame was residing
That trustfully followed Christ's guiding,
And now sees unveiled the salvation
It hoped for with glad expectation.

8 This body—O Earth, thou must shield it;
Now to thy safe keeping we yield it,
Till Christ comes again, to awake it
And like to His body to make it.

9 We praise Thee, and thank Thee, O Father,
That Thou Thine own children dost gather
To sleep after life's fitful story,
From sleep to the mansions of glory.

41

51   Jesus, Lover of My Soul.

Rev. Chas. Wesley.

Simeon B. Marsh.

FINE.

1. { Je - sus, lov - er of my soul,   Let me to Thy bo - som fly. }
{ While the near-er wa - ters roll.   While the tempest still is high; }
D. C.—*Safe in - to the ha - ven guide,*   Oh, *re-ceive my soul at last.*

2. { Oth - er ref - uge have I none,   Hangs my helpless soul on Thee; }
{ Leave, ah, leave me not a - lone,   Still sup-port and com-fort me. }
D. C.—*Cov - er my de-fence-less head,*   With *the shad-ow of Thy wing.*

Hide me, O my Sav - ior, hide.   Till the storm of life is past;
All my trust on Thee is stayed,   All my help from Thee I bring;

D. C.

3 Thou, O Christ, art all I want;
  More than all in Thee I find;
Raise the fallen, cheer the faint,
  Heal the sick, and lead the blind.
Just and holy is Thy name,
  I am all unrighteousness:
Vile, and full of sin I am,
  Thou art full of truth and grace.

4 Plenteous grace with Thee is found—
  Grace to cover all my sin:
Let the healing streams abound;
  Make and keep me pure within.
Thou of life the Fountain art,
  Freely let me take of Thee;
Spring Thou up within my heart,
  Rise to all eternity,

52   Around the Throne of God a Band!

John Mason Neale. 1866.

Francis Reginald Statham. 1844.

1. Around the throne of God a band Of glo-rious an - gels al - ways stand,
2. Some wait around Him, ready still To sing His praise and do His will;
3. Lord, give Thine angels ev - 'ry day Com-mand to guide us on our way;
4. So shall no wicked thing draw near To do us harm or cause us fear;

Bright things they see, sweet harps they hold, And on their heads are crowns of gold.
And some, when He commands them, go To guard His servants here be - low.
And bid them ev - 'ry eve-ning keep Their watch around us while we sleep;
And we shall dwell, when life is past, With angels round Thy throne at last.

53   Asleep in Jesus! Blessed Sleep.

MARGARET MACKAY.

JOSEPH CLAUDER. 1630.

1. A - sleep in Je - sus! bless-ed sleep, From which none ever wakes to weep;
2. A - sleep in Je - sus! O how sweet To be for such a slumber meet;
3. A - sleep in Je - sus! peaceful rest, Whose waking is su - preme-ly blest:
4. A - sleep in Je - sus! O, for me May such a bliss-ful ref-uge be:

A calm and un - dis - turbed re-pose, Un-bro-ken by the last of foes.
With ho - ly con - fi - dence to sing That death hath lost his ven-omed sting!
No fear, no woe shall dim that hour That man-i - fests the Sav-ior's power.
Se-cure - ly shall my ash - es lie, And wait the summons from on high.

54   Sun of My Soul.

JOHN KEBLE.

PETER RITTER.

1. Sun of my soul! Thou Sav-ior dear, It is not night if Thou be near:
2. When soft the dews of kind-ly sleep My wea-ried eye - lids gent - ly steep,
3. A - bide with me from morn till eve, For with-out Thee I can - not live;
4. Be near to bless me when I wake, Ere thro' the world my way I take;

Oh, may no earth-born cloud a - rise To hide Thee from Thy servant's eyes!
Be my last tho't—how sweet to rest For-ev - er on my Sav-ior's breast!
A - bide with me when night is nigh, For with-out Thee I dare not die.
A - bide with me till in Thy love I lose my - self in heav'n a-bove.

55   Abide, O Dearest Jesus.

Dr. J. STEGMANN.   MELCH. VULPIUS. 1609.

1. A - bide, O dear-est Je - sus, A - mong us with Thy grace,
2. A - bide, O dear Re - deem - er, A - mong us with Thy Word,
3. A - bide with heav'nly bright - ness, A - mong us, precious Light;
4. A - bide with rich-est bless - ings A - mong us, bounteous Lord;

That Sa - tan may not harm us, Nor we to sin give place.
And thus now and here - aft - er, True peace and joy af - ford.
Thy truth di - rect and keep us From err - or's gloom - y night.
Let us in grace and wis - dom Grow dai - ly through Thy Word.

5 Abide with Thy protection
   Among us, Lord our Strength;
Lest world and Satan fell us,
   And overcome at length.

6 Abide, O faithful Savior,
   Among us with Thy love,
Grant Steadfastness, and help us
   To reach our home above.

56   O Thou, Whose Own Vast Temple Stands.

FRANZ HAYDEN.

1. O Thou whose own vast tem - ple stands, Built o - ver earth and sea,
2. Lord, from Thine in - most glo - ry send, Within these courts to 'bide,
3. May err - ing minds that wor - ship here Be taught the bet - ter way;
4. May faith grow firm, and love grow warm, And pure de - vo - tion rise,

Ac - cept the walls that hu - man hands Have raised to wor - ship Thee!
The peace that dwell-eth with - out end, Se - ren - ly by Thy side!
And they who mourn, and they who fear, Be strengthened as they pray.
While round these hallowed walls the storm Of earth-born pas - sion dies.

57 A Slumber in Jesus' Name I Know.

MAGNUS BROSTRUP LANDSTAD. Died 1880.
Tr. from Norwegian by D. G. R. 1897.

C. E. F. WEISE. 1826.

1. A slum-ber in Je-sus name I know, A rest for the weary and weeping,
2. An evening hour with sun-set glow, I know, and I long to see it;
3. A morning I know so fair and bright, The angels shall sing God's praises,

A bed is made in the earth be-low, Se-cure as in moth-er's keep-ing,
For oft' on the way I'm faint and low, And the days are dark and drear-y
And Christ, God's anointed, shall come nigh And call as with thousand voic-es.

My soul is with God in heav'n a-bove And joys for its sor-row reap-ing.
Then longs my heart for the fall of day And a bliss-ful rest for the wea-ry.
He a-wak-ens us with His message sweet; The earth at His call re-joic-es.

4 So dear is the thought of this morn to me,
To my mind it often comes streaming
That with jubilant song I at last shall see
On the hill tops the golden dawn gleam-
    ing
As the little bird's sing in their happy glee,
In the Lindens at daybreaks beaming.

5 And Christ doth appear amidst angels
    throng,
His voice all peoples assemble;
Then crumbles to dust every fetter strong,
The depths of the ocean tremble,
He cries: "All ye dead ones arise, arise!"
In glory we God resemble!

6 And lo! there above is the gate ajar!
By name all the chosen are greeted.
Help God, on this day that Thy people we
    are;
That our dear ones in heaven we meeteth.
Oh, grant thro' the blood of Jesus Christ,
That in heaven we all may be seated.

7 Oh, Jesus, be near me when I die,
And touch me with tender blessing
And say that this maid, or this little boy
Is not dead, but is only sleeping.
Then trusting to Thee I rest till the day
When I wake in the land of the living.

45

58 Spread, O Spread Thou Mighty Word.

JONATHAN F. BAHNMAIER.   FREYLINGHAUSEN. 1704.

1. Spread, O spread, thou might-y Word, Spread the king-dom of the Lord,
2. Tell them how the Fa-ther's will Made the world and keeps it still;
3. Tell them of the Spir-it given Now, to guide us up to heav'n,

Where-so-e'er His breath has giv'n Life to be-ings ment for heav'n.
How He sent His Son to save All who help and com-fort crave.
Strong and ho-ly, just and true, Work-ing both to will and do.

4 Word of life, most pure and strong,
Lo, for Thee the nations long:
Spread, till from its dreary night
All the world awakes to light.

5 Lord of harvest, let there be
Joy and strength to work for Thee:
Let the nations far and near,
See Thy light and learn Thy fear.

59

1 Heaven and earth, and see and air,
All their Maker's praise declare:
Wake, my soul, awake and sing,
Now thy grateful praises bring.

2 See how He hath everywhere
Made this earth so rich and fair;
Hill and vale and fruitful land,
All things living show His hand.

3 See the waters ceaseless flow,
Ever circling to and fro:
From the sources to the sea,
Still it rolls in praise to Thee.

4 Lord, great wonders workest Thou!
To Thy sway all creatures bow:
Write Thou deeply in my heart
What I am and what Thou art.
JOACHIM NEANDER.

60   Had God Not Come.

MARTIN LUTHER.   Strasburg. 1525.

1. Had God not come, may Israel say, Had God not come to aid us,
   Our en-e-mies be-fore this day Would surely have dis-mayed us,
2. Their furious wrath, did God permit, Would surely have con-sumed us,
   And in the deep and yawning pit With life and limb en-tombed us;
3. Blest be the Lord, who from the pit Snatched us, when it was gap-ing;
   Our souls, like birds that break the net, To the blue skies es-cap-ing;

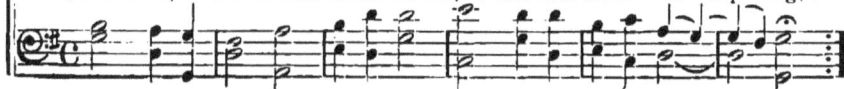

46

Had God Not Come.

For we are but a hand-ful small Held in con - tempt and
Like men o'er whom dark wa - ters roll, The streams had gone e'en
The snare is bro - ken— we are free! Our help is · ev - er,

scorn by all, All men rise up a - gainst us.
o'er our soul, And might - i - ly o'er - whelmed us.
Lord, in Thee, The God of earth and heav - - en.

61

1 Lord Jesus, Thou art truly good!
  Thou spreadst for our salvation
Thy body and Thy blood as food,
  And giv'st us invitation.
As weary souls, with sin oppressed,
We come to Thee for needed rest,
  For counsel and forgiveness.

2 Although Thou didst ascend to heaven,
  Where angels bow before Thee.
And now to mortals 'tis not given
  By sight here to adore Thee,
Until begins Thy judgment grand.
When we before Thy throne shall stand,
  And cheerfully behold Thee;

3 Yet art Thou ever with us. Lord,
  And with Thy congregation,
And not confined— so says Thy Word·—
  To any habitation.
Firm as a rock Thy Word still stands,
Unshaken by the en'mies' hands,
  Though they be e'er so cunning.

4 Thou say's: "This is my body; eat,
  And orally receive me!
This is my blood; drink all of it,
  And henceforth never leave me!"
What Thou hast spoken, true must be:
Thou art almighty, and with Thee
  Impossible is nothing.

5 Although my reason cannot see
  How in so many places
Thy body at a time may be,
  Yet faith Thy Word embraces.
How it can be I leave to Thee,
Thy Word alone sufficeth me,
  For Thou wilt that we trust it.

6 Lord, I believe in simple trust,
  Strength in my weakness give me
For I am naught but sinful dust,
  Nor of Thy word bereave me,
Thy Baptism, Supper. and Thy Word,
My consolation are, O Lord,
  For they contain my treasure.

7 Grant that we worthily receive
  Thy supper Lord, our Savior,
That for our sins we truly grieve,
  And prove by our behaviour
That we obtain Thy saving grace
And trust in it throughout our days;
  Then will our life be godly.

8 For Thy consoling Supper, Lord,
  Be praised throughout all ages!
Preserve it, for with one accord
  The world against it rages.
Grant that Thy body and Thy blood
May be my comfort and sweet food
  In my last moments. Amen

47

62 Jesus, Thy Blood and Righteousness.

NICOLAUS LUDWIG,
Count von Zinzendorf (1700-1760).   JOHN HATTON (—1793), 1790.

1. Je - sus, Thy Blood and right - eous - ness My beau - ty
2. Bold shall I stand in Thy great day, For who aught
3. This spot - less robe the same ap - pears, When ru - ined

are, my glo - rious dress; 'Midst flam - ing worlds, in
to my charge shall lay? Ful - ly through these ab -
na - ture sinks in years: No age can change its

these ar - rayed, With joy shall I lift up my head.
solved I am From sin and fear, from guilt and shame.
con - stant hue; Thy Blood pre - serves it ev - er new.

4 O let the dead now hear Thy voice;
Now bid Thy banished ones rejoice!
Their beauty this, their glorious dress,
Jesus, Thy Blood and Righteousness!

5 When from the dust of death I rise,
To claim my mansion in the skies,
Even then this shall be all my plea,
"Jesus hath lived and died for me."

63   Jesus, Still Lead On,

NICHOLAUS ZINZENDORF.   Darmstädter GES. BUCH. 1698

1. Je - sus, still lead on, Till our rest be won! And al-though the
2. If the way be drear, If the foe be near, Let not faith - less
3. When we seek re - lief From a long - felt grief; When temp-ta - tions
4. Je - sus, still lead on, Till our rest be won! Heav'nly Lead - er,

48

Jesus, Still Lead On.

way be cheer - less, We will fol - low, calm and fear - less.
fears o'er - take us, Let not faith and hope for - sake us;
come al - lur - ing, Make us pa - tient and en - dur - ing:
still di - rect us, Still sup - port, con - sole, pro - tect us,

Guide us by Thy hand To our Fa - ther - land!
For through ma - ny a foe To our home we go!
Show us that bright shore Where we weep no more!
Till we safe - ly stand In our Fa - ther - land!

64   A Babe is Born.

Anon.   Anon.

1. A Babe is born in Beth - le - hem, Beth - le - hem, There -
2. With-in a man - ger He doth lie, He doth lie, Whose
3. Still-ness was all the man - ger round, man - ger round, The

fore re - joice Je - ru - sa - lem. Hal - le - lu - jah! Hal - le - lu - jah!
throne is set a - bove the sky. Hal - le - lu - jah! Hal-le - lu - jah!
crea-ture its Cre - a - tor found. Hal - le - lu - jah! Hal-le - lu - jah!

4 The wise men came, led by the star, | 5 His mother is the Virgin mild,
Gold, myrrh, and incense brought from far. | And He the Father's only Child.

65   Children of the Heavenly King.

J. Cennic.

I. Pleyel.

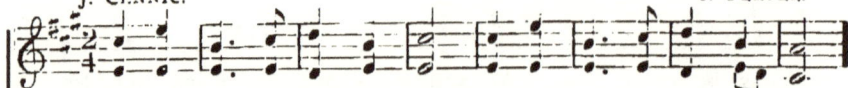

1. Children of the heav-'nly King, As we jour-ney, sweet-ly sing;
2. Ye are trav-'ling home to God In the way our fa-ther's trod;
3. Shout, ye lit-tle flock, and blest! You on Je-sus' throne shall rest;

Sing your Sav-ior's wor-thy praise, Glo-rious in His works and ways.
They are hap-py now, and ye Soon their hap-pi-ness shall see.
There your seat is now pre-par'd; There your kingdom and re-ward.

4 Fear not brethren; joyful stand
On the borders of your land;
Jesus Christ, your Father's Son,
Bids you undismay'd go on.

5 Lord, submissive make us go,
Gladly leaving all below;
Only Thou our Leader be,
And we still will follow Thee.

66   Weary of Earth.

Rev. Samuel John Stone.

E. Dearle.

1. Wea-ry of earth and la-den with my sin, I look to
2. It is the voice of Je-sus that I hear; His are the
3. 'Twas He who found me on the death-ly wild, And made me
4. Yea, Thou wilt an-swer for me Right-teous Lord; Thine all the

Heav'n and long to en-ter in, But there no e-vil
hands stretched out to draw me near, And His the blood that
heir of heav'n, the Fa-ther's child And day by day, where
mer-its, mine the great re-ward; Thine the sharp thorns, and

50

Weary of Earth.

thing may find a home; And yet I hear a voice that bids me "come."
can for all a - tone, And set me faultless there be - fore the throne.
by my soul may live, Gives me His grace of par-don, and will give.
mine the gold-en crown; Mine the life won; and Thine the life laid down.

67   America.

SAMUEL F. SMITH.   HENRY CAREY.

1. My coun-try, 'tis of thee, Sweet land of lib - er - ty,
2. My na - tive coun - try, thee— Land of the no - ble, free—
3. Let mu - sic swell the breeze, And ring through all the trees
4. Our Fa - thers' God! to Thee, Au - thor of lib - er - ty,

Of thee I sing: Land where my fa-thers died! Land of the
Thy name I love; I love thy rocks and rills, Thy woods and
Sweet free-dom's song; Let mor-tal tongues a - wake; Let all that
To Thee we sing: Long may our land be bright With free-dom's

Pil-grims' pride! From ev - 'ry moun - tain side Let free-dom reign.
tem - pled hills; My heart with rap - ture thrills Like that a - bove.
breathe partake; Let rocks their si - lence break,—The sound pro-long.
ho - ly light; Pro - tect us by Thy might, Great God, our King!

51

68   O Darkest Woe.

JOH. RIST.   Würzburger Gesbuch. 1628.

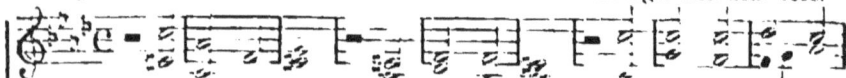

1. Oh, dark-est woe! Ye tears forth flow Has earth so sad a
2. O sor-row dread! Our God is dead, But by His ex-pi-
3. O child of man! It was the ban Of death on thee that

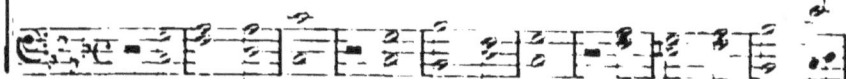

won - der: God the Father's on-ly Son, Now is car-ried yon-der.
a - tion Of our guilt up-on the cross Gained for us sal - va - tion.
brought Him Down to suf-fer for thy sins, And such woe hath wrought Him.

4 See, stained with blood,
The Lamb of God,
The Bridegroom lies before thee,
Pouring out His life that He
May to life restore thee.

5 O Ground of faith,
Laid low in death!
Sweet lips now silent sleeping!
Surely all that live must mourn
Here with bitter weeping.

69   Blessed Jesus, At Thy Word.

TOBIAS CLAUSNITZER.   JOHANN RUDOLPH AHLE. (1625-1673), 1664.

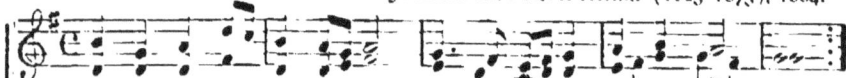

1. Bless-ed Je - sus, at Thy word We are gathered all to hear Thee;
   Let our heart and souls be stirred Now to seek and love and fear Thee;
2. All our knowledge, sense, and sight Lie in deepest dark-ness shroud - ed,
   Till Thy Spir - it breaks our night With the beams of truth un-cloud - ed,
3. Glorious Lord, Thy-self im - part! Light of light from God pro - ceed - ing,
   O - pen Thou our ears and heart, Help us by Thy Spir-it's plead - ing,

By Thy teachings, sweet and ho - ly, Drawn from earth to love Thee sole - ly.
Thou a - lone to God canst win us, Thou must work all good within us.
Hear the cry Thy peo - ple rais - es, Hear, and bless our pray'rs and prais - es.

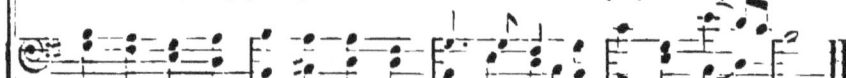

52

70 Jesus, Priceless Treasure.

JOH. FRANCK. 1653.   L. M. LINDEMAN. 1871.

1. Je - sus, price-less Treas-ure, Source of pur-est pleas-ure, Tru-est Friend to
2. In Thine arm I rest me, Foes who would molest me Can-not reach me
3. Sa-tan, I de - fy thee; Death, I need not fly thee; Fear, I bid thee

me! Long my heart hath pant - ed, Till it well nigh faint - ed,
here; Though the earth be shak - ing, Ev - 'ry heart be quak-ing,
cease! Rage, O world, thy nois - es Can - not drown our voic - es

Thirst-ing aft - er Thee! Thine I am O spot - less Lamb!
Je - sus calms my fear; Sin and hell in con - flict fell,
Sing-ing still of peace, For God's pow'r guards ev - 'ry hour;

I will suf - fer naught to hide Thee, Ask for naught be - side Thee.
With their heaviest storms assail me, Je - sus will not fail me.
Earth and all its depths a-dore Him, Si - lent bow be - fore Him.

71 Draw Nigh and Take the Body.

Tr. JOHN M. NEALE.   ARTHUR S. SULLIVAN.

1. Draw nigh and take the bod - y of the Lord,
2. Saved by the bod - y and that ho - ly blood,
3. Sal - va - tion's Giv - er, Christ, the on - ly Son,
4. Of - fered was He for great - est and for least,

And drink the ho - ly blood for you out - poured.
With souls re - freshed, we ren - der thanks to God.
By His dear cross and blood the vic - t'ry won.
Him - self the Vic - tim and Him - self the Priest.

5 Victims were offered by the law of old,
  That in a type celestial mysteries told.

6 He, Ransomer from death, and Light from shade,
  Now gives His holy grace, His saints to aid.

7 Approach ye then with faithful hearts sincere,
  And take the safeguard of salvation here.

8 With heavenly bread He makes the hungry whole,
  Gives living waters to the thirsting soul.

9 Alpha and Omega, to Whom shall bow
  All nations at the doom, is with us now.

72 O Lamb of God, Most Holy.

NIK. DECIUS.   BRAUNSCHWEIG KIRCH. ord. 1552.

1. { O Lamb of God most ho - ly! Who on the cross did lan - guish,
  { E'er pa-tient, meek and low - ly, Tho' mock'd amid Thine an - guish,

Our sins Thou learnest for us, Else would des - pair reign

54

O Lamb of God Most Holy.

o'er us! Have mer - cy on us, O Je - sus!
2. Have mer - cy on us, O Je - sus!
3. Thy grace be with us, O Je - sus!

73   I Come Unto Thy Manger Low.

P. GERHARDT.
Tr. from Ger. by D. G. R. 1897.   JOH. SEB. BACH. 1736.

1.{ I come un - to Thy man-ger low, O Je - sus, to a - dore Thee;
   { I come and bring and give Thee now What Thou in mer - cy gav'st me.
2.{ Be - fore I to this world was born, Thou wert un - to me giv - en,
   { And hast me chos-en as Thine own, Be - fore I knew Thee, e - ven.
3.{ In death's dark night I help - less lay, But Thou, my sun ap - pear-eth.
   { Thou art the sun that to me gave Light, life, and hope to cheer it.

Take it, it is my sense and soul, Heart,
Be - fore Thy hand me stat - ure gave Thy
O sun! that kin - dled in my heart The

spir-it, mood, O take it all, And let it on - ly please Thee!
heart in love pro - vis - ion made To give Thy - self un - to me.
light of faith, my sun Thou art, In glo - ry none is like Thee!

55

74   Come, Ye disconsolate.

T. Moore.   E. Pontoppidan's Hymnal. 1741.

{ Come, ye dis - con - so - late, wher - e'er ye lan - guish,
{ Here bring your wound-ed hearts, here tell your an - guish,

Come to the mer - cy sent, fer - vent - ly kneel; }
Earth hath no sor - row that heav'n can - not heal. } Joy of the

com-fort-less, Light of the stray - ing, Hope of the pen - i - tent

fade-less and pure; Here speaks the Com - fort - er, ten - der - ly

say - ing:—Earth hath no sor - row that heav'n can - not cure.

75 Come, Ye Disconsolate.

THOS. MOORE. Ver. 1 and 2.
THOS. HASTINGS. Ver. 3.

SAMUEL WEBBE.

1. Come, ye dis-con-so-late, wher-e'er ye lan-guish, Come to the
2. Joy of the com-fort-less, light of the stray-ing, Hope of the
3. Here see the Bread of life, see wa-ters flow-ing, Forth from the

mer-cy seat, fer-vent-ly kneel, Here bring your wounded hearts, here tell your
pen-i-tent, fade-less and pure; Here speaks the Com-fort-er, ten-der-ly
throne of God, pure from a-bove; Come to the feast of love: come, ev-er

an-guish; Earth hath no sor-row that heav'n can-not heal.
say-ing— Earth hath no sor-row that heav'n can-not cure.
know-ing Earth hath no sor-row but heav'n can re-move.

76

1 Brightest and best of the sons of the morning
Dawn on our darkness and lend us Thine aid:
Star of the East, the horizon adorning,
Guide where our infant Redeemer is laid.

2 Cold on His cradle the dew-drops are shining,
Low lies His head with the beasts of the stall:
Angels adore Him, in slumber reclining,
Maker, and Monarch, and Savior of all.

3 Say shall we yield Him, in costly devotion,
Odors of Edom, and offerings divine?
Gems of the mountains, and pearls of the ocean,
Myrrh from the forest, and gold from the mine?

4 Vainly we offer each ample oblation,
Vainly with gold would His favor secure:
Richer, by far, is the heart's adoration;
Dearer to God are the prayers of the poor.

R. HEBER.

57

77   All My Heart This Night Rejoices.

P. GERHARDT.   J. CRUGER. 1656.

1. All my heart this night re-joic - es, As I hear Far and
2. Forth to - day the Conqu'ror go - eth, Who the foe, Sin and
3. Shall we still dread God's dis-pleas - ure, Who to save Free-ly

near Sweetest an - gel voic - es; "Christ is born," their choirs are sing-
woe, Death and hell o'er-throw-eth, God is man, man to de - liv-
gave Us His dear - est treas - ure? To re - deem us, He hath giv -

ing. Till the air ev - 'ry-where, Now with joy is ring - ing.
er, His dear Son now is one With our blood for - ev - er.
en His own Son From the throne Of His might in heav - en.

4 Hark! a voice from yonder manger,
  Soft and sweet, Doth entreat:
"Flee from woe and danger;
  Brethren, from all ills that grieve you,
You are freed, All you need
I will surely give you."

5 Come, then, banish all your sadness,
  One and all, Great and small,
Come with songs of gladness;
  Love Him who with love is glowing.
Hail the Star Near and far
Light and joy bestowing!

78   Swell the Anthem.

NATHAN STRONG.   J, CRUGER. 1653.

1. Swell the an - them, raise the song, Prais-es to our God be-long;
2. Bless - ings from His liberal hand Flow a - round this hap - py land;
3. Here, be - neath a virtuous sway May we cheer - ful - ly o - bey;
4. Hark! the voice of nature sings Prais-es to the King of kings;

Swell the Anthem.

Saints and an-gels join to sing Prais - es to the heav'nly King.
Kept by Him no foes an - noy; Peace and free - dom we en - joy.
Nev - er feel op - pression's rod, Ev - er own and wor-ship God
Let us join the chor - al song, And the grate - ful notes pro - long.

79   Come, Descend, O Holy Spirit!

EHRENFRIED LIEBICH. Died 1780.
Tr. from Ger. by D. G. R. 1897.

J. CRUGER. 1653.

1. Come, de - scend, O Ho - ly Spir - it! Com-fort - er, Be us near,
2. Faith in God Thou hast cre - at - ed, Vain - ly do I pur - sue
3. Wake from sleep in sin the stray-ing! Hear to-day Those who may
4. High - est Spir - it, wise and ho - ly, Thro' Thy might, Give us light.

Fill Christ's church and cheer it! He, whose word was nev - er
Weal or woe un - aid - ed. And the work of souls' sal -
Be for coun - cil pray - ing. Snatch the world from its de -
That we God love sole - ly. Teach us to make our pe -

bro - ken, Made the vow: Spir - it Thou should annoint Thy peo - ple.
va - tion; None a - las, Pow-er has To ef - fect cre - a - tion.
struc - tion, And we pray That it may Heed Thy good in-struc - tion
ti - tions. When we pray, A - men say, Teach us true sub-mis - sion.

5 Help our faith to conquer evil;
    Put to shame By Thy name,
Flesh, world, sin and devil.
    Cross, or woe, or pain, or anguish.
None of it Do permit,
    Us from Christ to banish.

6 Might is Thine without denial;
    Be our stay That we may
Constant be in trial.—
    When our spirit God will sever
From this clay, Thee we pray:
    Give us joy forever!

80   Jerusalem, Thou City Fair.

JOHN M. MEYFART. Died 1642.   ERFURTER GES. BUCH. 1663.

1. Je - ru - sa - lem, thou cit - y fair and high, Would God I were in thee!
2. O   Zi - on, hail! Bright cit - y now un - fold The gates of grace to me!
3. Innumerous choirs be - fore the shining throne, Their joyful anthems raise,

My longing heart fain, fain to thee would fly! It will not stay with me;
How many a time   I longed for thee of old, Ere yet I   was set free
Till heav'n's glad halls are echoing with the tone Of that great hymn of praise,

Far o - ver vale and moun - tain, Far o - ver field and plain,
From yon dark life   of sad - ness, Yon world of shad - owy nought,
And all   its host re - joic - es, And all   its bless - ed throng

It   hastes to seek its Foun - tain And quit this world of pain.
And   God had given the glad - ness, The her - it - age I sought.
U - nite their myr - iad voic - es In one e - ter - nal song.

60

To Thee, O Lord. I yield my spir-it, Who break'st in love this mor - tal chain,
My life I but from Thee in-her-it, And death becomes my chief-est gain;

In Thee I live, in Thee I die, Content for Thou art ev - er nigh.

82

1 If thou but suffer God to guide thee,
And hope in Him through all thy ways,
He'll give thee strength whate'er betide thee,
And bear thee through the evil days;
Who trusts in God's unchanging love
Builds on the Rock that nought can move.

2 What can these anxious cares avail thee?
These never ceasing moans and sighs?
What can it help, if thou bewail thee
O'er each dark moment as it flies?
Our cross and trials do but press
The heavier for our bitterness.

3 Be only still, and wait His leisure
In cheerful hope, with heart content
To take whate'er our Father's pleasure
And all discerning love hath sent,
Nor doubt our inmost wants are known
To Him who chose us for His own.

4 He knows the time for joy, and truly
Will send it when He sees it meet,
When He has only tried us throughly,
And finds us free from all deceit,
Then cometh He all unaware,
And makes us own His loving care.

5 Nor think amid the heat of trial
That God hath cast thee off unheard,
That He whose hopes meet no denial
Must surely be of God preferred;
Time passes, and much change doth bring,
And sets a bound to every thing.

6 All are alike before the Highest;
'Tis easy to our God, we know,
To raise thee up, though low thou liest,
To make the rich man poor and low;
True wonders still by Him are wrought,
Who setteth up and brings to nought.

7 Sing, pray, and keep His ways unswerving,
Do but thine own part faithfully,
And trust His word; though undeserving,
Thou yet shalt find it true for thee;
God never will forsake in need
The heart that trusts in Him indeed.

NEUMARK.

61

83   Now Let Us Come Before Him!

P. Gerhardt.

Selnecker. 1587.

1. Now let us come be - fore Him, With songs and pray'rs a - dore Him,
2. The stream of years is flow - ing, And we are on - ward go - ing,
3. In woe we oft - en lan-guish, And pass thro' times of an - guish,
4. A faith - ful moth-er keep - eth Guard, while her in - fant sleep-eth,

Who to our life from heav - en All need-ed strength hath giv - en.
From old to new sur - viv - ing, And by His mer - cy thriv - ing.
Of wars and trep - i - da - tion, A - larm - ing ev - 'ry na - tion.
Its fear and grief as - suag - ing, When an - gry storms are rag - ing.

5 Thus God His children shieldeth
And full protection yieldeth;
When need and woes distress them,
His loving arms caress them.

6 In vain is all our doing;
The labor we're pursuing
In our hands prospers never,
Unless God watches ever.

7 Our song to Thee ascendeth,
Whose mercy never endeth;
Our thanks to Thee we render,
Who art our strong Defender.

8 O God of mercy! hear us,
Our Father! be Thou near us;
'Mid crosses and in sadness
Be Thou our Fount of gladness.

84   Draw Us to Thee!

Friedr. Funcke. Died 1699.

Chr. Peter. 1655.

1. Draw us to Thee, For then shall we Walk in Thy steps for-ev - er,
2. Draw us to Thee, Lord, lov-ing - ly; Let us de - part with glad-ness,
3. Draw us to Thee, O grant that we May find the road to heav - en;

Draw Us to Thee.

And has-ten on Where Thou art gone, To be with Thee, dear Sav - ior.
That we may be For - ev - er free From sorrow, grief, and sad - ness.
Di - rect our way, Lest we should stray, And from Thy paths be driv - en.

4 Draw us to Thee,
That also we
Thy heavenly bliss inherit,
And ever dwell
Where sin and hell
No more can vex our spirit.

5 Draw us to Thee
Unceasingly,
Into Thy kingdom take us;
Let us fore'er
Thy glory share,
Thy saints and joint-heirs make us.

85   Arisen is the Holy Christ.

(Surrexit Christus hodie.)

Tr. by D G. R. 1897.   Ancient. Acc. to M. WEISSE. 1531.

1. A - ris - en is the ho - ly Christ! Hal - le - lu - jah! Hal-le - lu - jah!
2. And if the grave had held Him bound, Hal - le - lu - jah! Hal-le - lu - jah!
3. But now, since He a-rose from death, Hal - le - lu - jah! Hal-le - lu - jah!

For our sins He was sac - ri - ficed; Hal - le - lu - jah! Hal - le - lu - jah!
The world had not sal - va - tion found, Hal - le - lu - jah! Hal - le - lu-jah!
We praise Thee Christ without re-gret. Hal - le - lu - jah! Hal - le - lu jah!

4 O Jesus, dearest God and Lord,
Hallelujah! Hallelujah!
In need us help, from sin us guard;
Hallelujah! Hallelujah!

5 Help us that we from death arise,
Hallelujah! Hallelujah!
And be with Thee in Paradise!
Hallelujah! Hallelujah!

63

86   O Blest the House.

Chr. K. L. von Pfeil. Died 1784.   Wolder, Hamburg. 1598.

1. O blest the house, whate'er be-fall, Where Je - sus Christ is all   in all;
2. O blest that house, where faith ye find, And all with - in have set their mind
3. O blest the par - ents who give heed Un - to their children's foremost need,

Yea, if He were not dwell-ing there, How poor, and dark, and void it were.
To trust their God and serve Him still, And do in all His ho - ly will.
And wea - ry not of care or cost: To them and heav'n shall none be lost.

4 Blest such a house, it prospers well,
In peace and joy the parents dwell,
And in their children's lot is shown
How richly God can bless His own.

5 Then here will I, and mine to-day
A solemn cov'nant make and say:
Though all the world forsake Thy Word,
I and my house will serve the Lord.

87

1 This child we dedicate to Thee,
O God of grace and purity!
Shield it from sin and threatening wrong,
And let Thy love its life prolong.

2 Oh, may Thy Spirit gently draw
Its willing soul to keep Thy Law,
May virtue, piety, and truth.
Dawn even with its dawning youth.

3 We too, before Thy gracious sight,
Once shared the blest baptismal rite,
And would renew its solemn vow
With love, and thanks, and praises, now.

4 Grant that, with true and faithful heart,
We still may act the Christian's part,
Cheered by each promise Thou hast given,
And laboring for the prize in heaven.

S. Gillman.

88   From Thee, O God, Comes Ev'ry Favor.

Kaspar Neumann. Died 1715.
Tr. from Ger. by D. G. R. 1897.   Wagner. 1742.

1. From Thee, O God, comes ev'ry fa - vor, Thy household is the whole great world
2. For countless hosts Thou spreads't Thy ta - ble Each day with countless gifts of love.
3. We sow the seed, Thou growth be-stow-est; We work but Thou prepar'st the fruit;

64

From Thee, O God, Comes Ev'ry Blessing.

Thou spread'st Thy gifts as does a fa - ther, Be - fore all liv-ing, young and old.
No heart, no mind, no soul is a - ble To comprehend Thy stores a-bove:
The winds that waft thro' field and for-rest, The clouds, the rain, and heaven's dew,

Pro - vis - ion Thou hast made for all, For mor - tal bod - y, liv-ing soul.
For ev - 'ry soul in ev - 'ry land Is fed and nourished by Thy hand.
The sun-rays,- all Thy serv-ants are To do Thy bid-dings near and far.

89   It is Not Death to Die.

Dr. C. HENRY ABRAHAM, Malan.   GEORGE FRIEDRICH HANDEL.
1787-1864.   1685-1759.

1. It is not death to die, To leave this wea - ry road, And,
2. It is not death to close The eye long dimmed with tears! And,
3. It is not death to bear The wrench that sets us free From

'midst the broth - er-hood on high, To be at home with God.
wake in glo - ri - ous re - pose To spend e - ter - nal years.
dun - geon chain, to breathe the air Of bound-less lib - er - ty.

4 It is not death to fling   5 Jesus, Thou Prince of Life,
   Aside the sinful dust,   Thy chosen cannot die;
   And rise on strong, exulting wing,   Like Thee, they conquer in the strife,
   To live among the just.   To reign with Thee on high.

90   What Our Father Does is Well.

SAM. RODIGAST. Died 1708.   J. G. EBELING. 1666.

1. { What our Fa - ther does is well, Bless - ed truth His . chil - dren tell!
{ Tho' He send, for plen - ty, want, Tho' the har - vest - store be scant,

2. { What our Fa - ther does is well: Shall the wil - ful heart re - bel
{ If a bless - ing He with - hold In the field, or in the fold? }

Yet we rest up - on His love, Seek - ing bet - ter things a - bove.
Is He not Him - self to be All our store e - ter - nal - ly?

3 What our Father does is well:
Though He sadden hill and dell,
Upward yet our praises rise
For the strength His Word supplies.
He has called us sons of God;—
Can we murmur at His rod?

4 Therefore unto Him we raise
Hymns of glory, songs of praise:
To the Father and the Son
And the Spirit, Three in One,
Honor, might, and glory be,
Now and through eternity.

91   O Dearest Jesus, Thee I Pray.

B. HELDER. 1614.   HEINR. EGLI. 1786.

1. O dear - est Je - sus, Thee I pray: With - in my heart now make Thy stay,
2. Thou art my life and hap - pi - ness, Whom God hath sent, my soul to bless:
3. Lord, with Thy light show me the way, That nev - er I may go a - stray;
4. Lift up Thy face up - on me, Lord, In life and death Thy help af - ford;

That I, like Si - me - on of old, By faith may glad - ly Thee in - fold.
O cleanse and pur - i - fy my heart, That from Thy paths I ne'er de - part.
Ward off all sor - row and des - pair, And let me be Thine own for - e'er.
Then I'll de - part most cheer - ful - ly This life, when - e'er it pleas - eth Thee.

92   Awake Thou Spirit.

K. H. v. Bogatzky. (1st, 3d, 4th and 6th v.)   Konr. Kocher. 1855,

1. A - wake Thou Spirit, who didst fi - re   The god-like watchmen
2. Lord, let our ear-nest pray - er be heard,   The pray'r Thy Son our
3. O haste, O Lord, to help ere we are lost!   Send preachers forth in
4. And let Thy blessed word have speedy course,   Through ev - 'ry land be

of the Church's youth, Who faced the foes' en-ven - omed ire,
Lord, hath bid us pray, For lo, Thy children's hearts are stirred
spir - it sound and strong, Arm'd with Thy sword, the Word, a dauntless host,
blessed and glo - ri - fied, Till all the heathens know its saving force,

Who boldly preach'd both day and night Thy truth, Whose mighty voic - es
In ev - 'ry land on eatth, in this our day,, To cry with fer-vent
Bold to at - tack and crush the rule of wrong; Let them the earth for
And come and fill Thy church - es far and wide; A-wake, old Is - rael

loud are ringing still, And still are bringing hosts to know Thy will.
heart and soul to Thee, O say Thy A-men, Lord! So let it be.
Thee a-lone re-claim, Thy her - it-age to know and hail Thy name.
from its sleep O Lord, And read, O spread the con - quest of Thy Word!

67

93   Be True to God.

MICH. FRANCK. Tr. from Ger. by D. G. R. 1897.   MICH. FRANCK. 1637.

1. Keep faith-ful-ly the promise Thou Hast made in con - fir - ma - tion,
2. Be true to God, let troub-le not Nor cross thee from Him sev - er,
3. Be true to God, what - ev - er be Your call or rank or sta - tion.
4. Be true to God, con-fess His name, His word thou hear and hon - or,

Make in thy life this sa - cred vow Thy bulwark and foun - da - tion,
If He's thy Fa - ther and thy God, Canst thou then have it bet - ter?
What harm can come, if on - ly He Has thee in His pro - tec - tion?
Be steadfast; let no fear nor fame Nor place af-fect this man - ner.

Re-mem-ber that God prom-ised hath In thy baptismal hour,
This hight-est good Gives hap-py mood Hast thou His grace and pleasure,
A for-tress is His bless-ed grace 'Gainst world and sin and dev - il,
The world will have Its dust and chaff; They shall to-geth-er per - ish,

To lead and guard, And thee award A father's love for-ev - - er.
O hap-py soul, Then hast thou more Than heav'n or earth can meas - ure.
His standard can Mis-lead no man, But shields from ev'ry e - vil.
But God's own word Shall still go forth And without failure flour - - ish.

94   One Thing's Needful!

J. H. SCHROEDER. 1699.   JOH. SEB. BACH. 1736.

1. { One thing's needful! then Lord Je-sus, Keep this one thing in my mind; }
   { All be-side, though first it please us, Soon a griev-ous yoke we find; }

2. { Soul, wilt thou this one thing find thee? Seek not 'midst cre - at - ed things; }
   { What is earth - ly, leave be-hind thee, O - ver na - ture stretch thy wings. }

3. { Thus my longings, heav'n-ward tending, Je - sus, rest a - lone on Thee; }
   { Help me, thus on Thee de-pend-ing, Sav - ior, come and dwell in me! }

4. { Therefore, Je - sus, my Sal - va-tion, Thou my One, my All, shalt be, }
   { Prove my fixed de - ter - mi-na - tion, Root out all hy - poc - ri - sy; }

Be - neath it the heart is still fret-ting and striv-ing, No true, last-ing
For where God and Man both in One are u - nit - ed, With God's per fect
Al-though all the world should forsake and for - get Thee, In love I will
Look well if on sin's slippery paths I am hast-ing, And lead me, O

hap - pi - ness ev - er de - riv - ing, The gain of this one thing all
ful - ness the heart is de - light - ed, There.there is the worth-i - est
fol-low Thee, ne'er will I quit Thee; Lord Je - sus, both spir - it and
Lord, in the way ev - er - last - ing! This one thing is need - ful, all

loss can re - quite, And teach me in all things to find true de - light.
lot and the best, My One and my All, and my Joy and my Rest.
life is Thy Word; And is there a joy which Thou dost not af - ford?
oth - ers are vain; I count all but loss that I Christ may ob - tain.

69

95   Thy Little Ones Are Coming Now.

H. A. Brorson. Died 1764.
Tr. from Nor. by D. G. R. 1897.

1. Thy lit-tle ones are com-ing now, O Je-sus, to Thy man-ger low. Pour
2. With songs we hasten Thee to meet, To kiss the dust be-fore Thy feet. O
3. O wel-come from the blissful spheres In heaven, to this vale of tears, Where

out Thy light on heart and mind That we the way to Thee may find.
hap-py hour, O bless-ed night! O welcome Thou, our hearts' de-light!
naught was tendered Thee by us, But sta-ble, pov-er-ty and cross.

4 How can it be, O Lord, that, still
To-day, so few consider well
Thy boundless love, O Jesus Christ,
Who for our sake all sacrificed?

5 Draw us to Thee! we pray again,
O Child of God, our Lord and Friend;
That Thee we, through Thy saving grace,
In holy love and faith embrace!

6 Against the world, protection grant!
Help us baptism's covenant
With holy zeal sacred to keep,
Our hearts for Thee in love to beat!

7 To-day we are a little band
Who humbly at Thy manger stand.
Help. that in countless hosts we may
Be near Thy throne on judgment day!

96   I Am Content.

MARTIN GRUNWALD.
Tr. from Ger. by D. G. R. 1897.   B. REIMANN. 1747.

1. I am con-tent this world to leave, It promis's well, but scant-ly gives.
2. In righteousness He has me dress'd, Yet oft-en times I am dis-tress'd:
3. And when the spir-it does in-sist 'Gainst sin to stand, flesh to re-sist,
4. Were I, O Je-sus Christ, with Thee, I should the ho-ly an-gels see!

70

I Am Content.

At most its gift is an-guish sore; And did it ev - er prom - ise more!
My lit - tle faith the foe as - sail, In prayer, con - stan-cy me fail,
They oft ef - fect my o - ver-throw, And humble me be - fore the foe;
Yea, e - ven I should sing Thy praise; With all the saints proclaim Thy grace.

It was a vis - ion - a - ry boon. O wert I Lord, in heav - en soon.
In ho-li - ness of life I see That lit - tle I re - sem - ble Thee.
Therefore the Spir - it cries in me: O that I were in heav'n with Thee!
O God, my Lord who gave me soul, I long to hear Thy fi - nal call!

97   Our Heavenly Father.

J. MONTGOMERY.   1210 acc. to T. G. STORL. Died 1730.

1. Our heav'n-ly Fa - ther, hear The pray'r we of - fer now;
2. Thy king - dom come; Thy will On earth be done in love,
3. Our dai - ly bread sup - ply While by Thy word we live;

Thy name be hallowed far and near, To Thee all Na-tions bow.
As saints and ser - a - phim ful - fill Thy ho - ly will a - bove.
The guilt of our in - iq - ui - ty For - give as we for - give.

4 From dark temptation's power,
   From Satan's wiles, defend;
   Deliver in the evil hour,
   And guide us to the end.

5 Thine shall forever be
   Glory and power divine;
   The scepter, throne, and majesty,
   Of heaven and earth are Thine.

98   The Grace of the Lord.

2 Cor. 13 : 14.

GOTTLOB HILMER. 1784. (or Christ Gregor.)

1. The grace of the Lord Je - sus Christ, And the love of God. And the com - mun-ion of the Ho - ly Ghost Be with us all, Be with us all. A - a - men.

99   Bless, O Lord, and Keep Us.

Acc. to Numbers 6 : 24-26 by D. G. R.

CHRIST. GREGOR. 1784.

1. Bless, O Lord and keep us Through Thy lov - ing kind - ness!
2. Peace up - on us show - er By Thy sav - ing pow - er!
3. A - men, say, O Fa - ther! Je - sus Christ, us gath - er

Lift Thy face up - on all Thine! Let it, Lord, up - on us shine!
Lift Thy coun - te - nance. O Lord, On us through Thy bless-ed Word!
By Thy grace in - to Thy fold! Ho - ly Spir - it, guide us all!

72

Salmer for Sondagsskolen.

1 Mel. Eng. Hymn No. 22.

1 Ophold os, Gud og Fader kjær,
  I Katechismi rene Lær',
  Som du ved Luther lod udgaa
  For de Enfoldige og Smaa.

2 Forlen os Naade her paa Jord,
  At holde ret de ti Bud-Ord;
  Forlen os, Herre, Troen skjøn
  Til Jesum Christ, din kjære Søn!

3 Vor Fader, som os hjælpe kan,
  Vi bede dig i Jesu-Navn,
  Hjælp os at tænke paa vor Daab
  Og leve og dø i Livsens Haab!

4 Og falde vi, lad os opstaa
  Og gjøre Bod og Naade faa
  Og nyde saa dit Kjød og Blod
  Alt under Brød og Vinen god!

5 Ophold os Herre, Helligaand,
  I Levnet rent og Lærdom sand,
  Stat os bi udi alskens Nød
  Og frels os fra den evig' Død!

2 Mel. Eng. Hymn No. 3.

Aabne, Jesu, du vort Øre,
Og oplys du vor Forstand,
At dit salig' Ord vi høre
Og i Hjertet gjemme kan!
Ved din Aand den Naade giv,
At det virker Tro og Liv,
Saa vort ganske Levnet kunde
Prise dig i alle Stunde!

3 Mel. Eng. Hymn No. 3.

Skriv dig, Jesu, paa mit Hjerte,
O min Konge og min Gud,
At ei Vellyst eller Smerte
Dig formaar at slette ud!
Denne Indskrift paa mig sæt:
Jesus udaf Nazareth,
Den Korsfæstede, min Ære
Og min Salighed skal være!

4 Mel. Eng. Hymn No. 17.

O, Jesu gid du vilde
Mit Hjerte danne saa,
Det baade aarle og silde,
Dit Tempel være maa;
Du selv min Hjerne vende
Fra Verdens kloge Flok,
Og lær mig dig at kjende,
Saa har jeg Visdom nok.

5 Mel. Eng. Hymn No. 69.

1 Lover Herren! han er nær,
  Naar vi synge, naar vi bede,
  Samles i hans Navn vi her,
  Er han midt blandt os tilstede.
  Lover Herren, Gamle, Unge,
  Pris hans Navn hver Barnetunge!

2 Herre, vær os evig nær!
  Vær os nær, naar Sol oprinder,
  Og naar Sol og Stjerneskjer
  I den dybe Nat forsvinder;
  Lad din Aand ei fra os vige,
  Til vi se dig i dit Rige!

6 Mel. Eng. Hymn No. 12.

Guds Ord, det er vort Arvegods,
Det skal vor Afkoms være;
Gud giv os i vor Grav den Ros,
Vi holdt det høit i Ære!
Det er vor Hjælp i Nød.
Vor Trøst i Liv og Død:
O Gud, ihvor det gaar,
Lad dog, mens Verden staar,
Det i vor Æt nedarves!

7 Mel. Eng. Hymn No. 12.

Sign Ordet i de Unges Mund,
Dets Kraft i Hjertet brænde.
At de vor Tro og Troens Grund
Sandfærdig maa bekjende!
Engang de bares frem,
Og du velsigned dem,
Du tog de Smaa i Favn,
De døbtes i dit Navn,
O, kjendes ved dem, Herre!

8 Mel. Eng. Hymn No. 26.

1 O, du trefoldig Enighed,
  Og en sand Gud af Evighed!
  Om Solen bort med Dagen gaar,
  Dit Guddoms Lys dog hos os staar.

2 Vi love dig om Morgenstund,
  Om Aftenen bede om din Miskund;
  Vor arme Lovsang prise dig;
  Thi du er god evindelig.

3 Gud Fader evig Ære ske,
  Guds Søn, som frelste os fra Ve,
  Og Aanden, som os trøste kan,
  Ske Lov og Pris i alle Land.

9 Mel. Eng. Hymn No. 69.

Nu vor Gjerning her er endt,
Og Velsignelsen vi eie,
Er vort Sind til Hjemmet vendt,
Der vi vil paa Herrens Veie
Efterleve, hvad vi lære,
Herrens Navn til Lov og Ære.

2 Følg saa med os ud og ind,
Hjertefromme Gud og Fader!
Hold ved Ordet fast vort Sind,
Saa vi aldrig dig forlader,
Men, naar Verdens Strid er omme,
Vi til dig i Himlen komme.

10 Mel. Eng. Hymn No. 3.

Lov og Tak og evig Ære
Ske dig, Guds enbaarne Søn,
Som en Tjener vilde være,
Kommen udaf David's Kjøn:
Søde Jesu! lær du mig,
At jeg vandrer rettelig,
Og i dine Fodspor træder,
Ja udi din Vei mig glæder.

2 Lad mig aldrig dig forsage,
Om end Kors og Kummer mig
Skal i denne Verden plage,
Men at jeg dog hjertelig
Elsker dig indtil min Død,
Og forlindrer al min Nød
Med din Fødsel, Død og Smerte:
Tag dem aldrig fra mit Hjerte.

11 Mel. Eng. Hymn No. 7.

1 Op alle, som paa Jorden bor,
Og takker Gud med mig,
Hvis Lov i helligt Englekor
Udsjunges idelig!:||:

2 Han giver Helbred, Liv og Brød
Os alle ufortjent;
I megen Angest, Sorg og Nød
Har han os Hjælp tilsendt.:||:

3 Skjønt vi ham tidt fortørnet har,
Han dog langmodig er
Og gjør, at vi for Straffen faar
Endog Velgjerninger.:||:

4 Han giver os et Hjerte fro
Og sand Frimodighed,
At vi kan tjene ham med Ro
I Verdens Vildsomhed.:||:

5 Vort Øie han selv lukker til
I Dødens fæle Nat,
Og naar vort Hjerte briste vil,
Er han vor Del og Skat.:||:

12 Mel. Eng. Hymn No. 30.

1 Lov, Ære, Pris og Herlighed
Gud Fader ske i Evighed,
Som Alting skabte viselig,
Og os opholder rigelig!

2 Dig Ære ske, o Jesu Christ,
Som har den Naade os bevist,
For os at lide Korsets Død,
Og frelste os af al vor Nød!

3 Dig Ære ske, o Helligaand,
Som tænder Lys i vor Forstand,
At Sandheds Ord vi fatte maa
Og fast' i det til Enden staa!

4 O hellige Treenighed,
O sande Gud i Evighed,
Hør os ved din Barmhjertighed,
Før os til evig Salighed!

13 Mel. Eng. Hymn No. 14.

1 Hvor lifligt er det dog at gaa
Med Jesu Ord i Munde,
Hans Saar, hans Død at tænke paa,
Og alt hans Verk begrunde!

2 O Jesu, o du ved, jeg gaar,
Din Pillegrim og Borger,
I disse korte Verdens Aar
Fuld af ti tusind Sorger!

3 Du est dog al mit Hjertes Ro,
Min Trøst, min daglig Tale,
O lad din Aand mit Hjertes Bo
Med al din Pinsel male!

4 Dig vandrer jeg saa gjerne med,
Opstandne Jesu milde,
Til Himlen jeg i dine Fjed
Saa gjerne følges vilde!

14 Mel. Eng. Hymn No. 7.

1 O tænk, naar engang samles skal
De frelstes Menighed
Af alle Folkeslægters Tal
I Himlens Herlighed!:||:

2 O tænk, naar Herrens Vidnehær,
Hans Tjenere paa Jord,
De Millioner møde der,
Som hørte deres Ord!:||:

3 O tænk dog, hvilken Jubellyd—
En Strøm af Kjærlighed!
Tænk, hvilken Tak og Pris og Fryd
Og Salighed og Fred!:||:

4 O Gud, hvad er din Naade stor!
Os alle til dig drag,
At vi kan staa blandt Frelstes Kor
Paa denne Høitidsdag!:||:

74

15 Mel. Eng. Hymn No. 39.

1 Min Sjæl er glad i Himlens Gud,
Sit Barn han kalder mig;
Han giver mig sit Ord og Bud
Og leder mig til sig.

2 Han har mig sagt, at arm jeg var,
Hvis han ei var mig god;
Men Omsorg for sit Barn han har.
For mig randt Jesu Blod.

3 I Daaben tog han mig imod
Han toed' ren min Sjæl,
Det blev mig gjort for Lammets Blod,
Gud vilde mig saa vel.

4 Saa er jeg det, han kalder mig:
Hans Barn, hans Eiendom;
Og derfor gaar til ham min Vei,
Naar jeg er god og from.

16. Mel. Eng. Hymn No. 37.

1 Hjælp,Jesu,hjælp,at jeg din Naade finder!
Udi dit Navn et nyt Aar jeg begynder,
Ak, lad det mig til Gavn og dig til Ære
Velsignet være.

2 Hjælp, Jesu,hjælp,og med din Aand mig styrke,
At jeg maa dig af ganske Hjerte dyrke,
Mod verdens Svig og Djævlens Anløb stride,
Mit Sind at bryde!

3 Hjælp, Jesu, hjælp, at jeg maa taalig være,
Naar jeg og dette Aar skal Korset bære,
Lad mig ei fristes over min Formue,
Men Frelsning skue!

4 Hjælp, Jesu, hjælp,at haabe,tro og bede,
Og mine Synder daglig at begræde,
Dit Ord betragte, derved i mit Hjerte,
Faa Trøst i Smerte!

17 Mel. Eng. Hymn No. 22.

1 Herre Gud, du som min Fader est,
Jeg beder dig ved Jesum Christ,
Paa hans Ord, Ed og haarde Død,
Hør os og hjælp i Angst og Nød!

2 Giv os dit Ord og styrk vor Aand,
Saa vi dig villig tjene kan,
Giv Venner, Fred og dagligt Brød,
Bevar vort Land fra alskens Nød!

3 Fri os fra Djævel, Synd og Død,
Fra Legemets og Sjælens Nød,
En salig Time mig beskjær,
Dit Riget, Magten, Æren er!

4 Amen, o Gud, i Jesu Navn,
Ophold min Tro til evigt Gavn,
Du est alene Fader min,
Gjør mig til Barn og Arving din!

18 Mel. Eng. Hymn No. 57.

1 Den signede Dag, som vi nu se.
Ned til os af Himmelen komme,
Gud lyser for os jo længer og mer
Os alle til Glæde og Fromme!
Gud lade os ikke ske idag
Last, Skam eller nogen Vaande!

2 Gud Fader og Søn og Helligaand
Med alle sine Engleskare,
Bevare os idag og allen Stund
For alskens Djævelens Snare,
Fra al den Avind, han til os bær
Vor Sjæl og vort Legem til Fare!

3 Det Kors, vor Herre han bar for os,
For vor Synd og ikke for sine,
Det sætter jeg idag mellem Djævlen og mig,
Jeg mener Guds værdige Pine;
Det Blod, der ned paa Korset randt,
Det slukker ud Synder mine.

4 Om levende blev hvert Træ i Skov,
Og var saa hvert Blad en Tunge,
Og havde de Maal, og kunde Guds lov
Med Englenes Stemme sjunge.
Tilfulde de dog vor Herre ei
Ret love og prise kunde.

5 Det er vel fuldt ondt med liden Magt
Mod høie Bjerge at springe,
Men Fuglen den lille naar sin Agt,
Naar Veiret bær under hans Vinge;
Saa hjælper og os Guds Aand fuldgod
Vor Frelser et Tak at bringe.

19 Mel. Eng. Hymn No. 22.

1 O himmelske Gud og Fader blid,
Vi takke dit Navn i allen Tid,
At du har hidtil naadelig
Os vogtet vel for Djævelens Svig.

2 Vi bede dig og for Christi Død,
Bevar os fra al Jammer og Nød,
Bevogt os med din Englehær
Og med din Aand du os regjer!

3 Vor Fa'er og Mo'er bevar du saa,
De længe med os leve maa,
Lad os opvoxe i Ære og Dyd
Og Gudsfrygt være vores Pryd!

4 Giv os godt Nemme og Forstand.
At lære, hvad dig tækkes kan,
Lad i vor Daabes-Pagt os staa,
Saalænge vi i Verden gaa.

5 Lad Synd og Sorg ei hos os bo,
Giv os i Dag din Fred og Ro,
Vi Sjæl og Liv befale dig,
Saa vaage og sove vi tryggelig.

20 Nu Solen gaar ned.

1. Nu So - len gaar ned, Og Af - te - nen bre - der paa
2. Hav Tak for i - dag, Gud Fa - der i Him - len, Som
3. For - lad mig, min Gud, Hvad jeg ha - ver syn - det i -
4. Jeg ved, du det gjør Jeg sluk - ker mit Lys og til -

Jor - den sin Fred, Smaa-fu - gle - ne fly - ve til Re - der - ne hen,
frem-med min Sag! Du har mig om heg - net, alt Ondt fra mig vendt,
mod di - ne Bud! Du prø - ver mit Hjer - te og kjen - der mit Pund,
luk - ker min Dør, Og sø - ger mit Lei - e og læg - ger mig ned,

Og Blom - sten har luk - ket sit Oi - e i - gjen Saa
Mit Ar - beid vel - sig - net, mig Lyk - ke til - sendt, Saa
Du hør - te hvert Ord, der gik ud af min Mund; Lad
Gud la - de mig sø - de - lig so - ve i Fred! Dig,

luk - ke mit Hjer-te med Laa - ge i Løn En gu - de - lig Bøn.
mil - de - lig Ti - mer-ne for mig hen-randt, Tak ske dig saa sandt!
væ - re, hvad der - i var syn - digt og slemt, Til - giv - et og glemt!
Je - su be - fal - er jeg trø - stig i Haand Mit Le - gem og Aand!

21   I Dag opstod den Herre Krist.

1. I   Dag op - stod den   Her - re Krist,   Den   Her - re   Krist,   Til
2. Som for - dags led den   bit - tre Død,   Den   bit - tre Død,   At
3. I   Kvin-der, som her   ban - ge staa,   Her   ban - ge staa,   Til
4. Dis - cip - le - ne det   si - ger der,   Det   si - ger der,   Op-

al - le Slæg-ters Trøst for-vist.   Hal - le - lu - ja,   Hal - le - lu - ja!
.fri os Men-ne - sker   af Nød.   Hal - le - lu - ja,   Hal - le - lu - ja!
Ga - li - læ - a   skal I gaa,   Hal - le - lu - ja,   Hal - le - lu - ja!
stan-den Æ - rens Kon - ge er.   Hal - le - lu - ja,   Hal - le - lu - ja!

5 I denne Paaskens glade Tid,
Den glade Tid,
Vi ville love Herren blid.
Halleluja, Halleluja!

6 Gud Fader, Søn og Helligaand,
Og Helligaand,
Nu være Tak i alle Land!
Halleluja, Halleluja!

22   Det kimer nu til Julefest.

1. Det ki - mer nu til   Ju - le - fest, Det ki - mer for den   høi - e Gjest,
2. O kom - mer med til   Da - vids By, Hvor En - gle syn - ge   un - der Sky;
3. O lad os gaa med   stil - le Sind Som Hyr - der - ne til   Bar - net ind,

Som steg til la - ve   Hyt - te ned Med   Nyt - aars - Ga-ver, Fryd og Fred.
O, kommer med paa   Mar - ken ud,   Hvor   Hyr - der hø - re Nyt fra Gud!
Med Glæ-des-taa - rer   tak - ke Gud For   Mi-skund-hed   og Naa-de-bud.

23 **Glade Jul.**

1. Gla - de Jul, hel - li - ge Jul! Eng - le da - le ned i Skjul,
2. Jul - e - fryd, e - vig Fryd, San - ge fuld' af him-melsk Lyd!
3. Fred paa Jord, Fryd paa Jord; Je - sus-bar - net blandt os bor!
4. Sa - lig Fred, him-melsk Fred! To - ner Ju - le - nat her - ned;

Hid de fly - ve med Pa - ra-dis-grønt, Hvor de se, hvad for Gud er skjønt,
Det er En - gle, som Hyr-der - ne saa, Dengang Her - ren i Kryb ben laa,
En - gle sjun - ge om Bar-net saa smukt. Han har Himmerigs Dør op-lukt,
En - gle brin - ge til Sto - re og Smaa Bud om ham, som i Kryb-ben laa,

Løn - lig i-blandt os de gaa, Løn - lig i-blandt os de gaa.
E - vig er En - gle-nes Sang: E - vig er En - lge-nes Sang.
Sa - lig er En - gle-nes Sang; Sa - lig er En - gle-nes Sang.
Fryd dig, hver Sjæl, han har frelst; Fryd dig, hver Sjæl, han har frelst.

24 **O Jesu! havde vi ei dig.**

1. O Je - su! hav - de vi ei dig, Var du ei kom - men hid,
2. Thi Syn - den os i Vei - en stod; Fra den vi ren - ses maa,
3. Jeg er saa glad og tak - ker dig, At du til Jor - den kom;

O Jesu! havde vi ei dig.

Saa var til - luk - ket Him - me - rig, Og al - drig kom vi did.
Der - for har du ud - øst dit Blod, At vi kan Ren-hed faa.
Din Kjær-lig - hed skal hol - de mig, Naar Ver-den fal - der om.

25   Jeg hörte i en sagte Lyd.

1. Jeg hør - te i en sag - te Lyd Min Frel - sers mil - de Røst:
2. Jeg kom til Je - sus, som jeg var, E - len - dig, fuld af Nød;
3. Jeg hør - te at - ter Je - su Røst, "Se, hvad jeg giv - er dig:
4. Jeg kom til Je - sus, og jeg drak Af Naa-dens Kil - de - væld—

Læg ned, du Træt - te, kom, læg ned Dit Ho - ved til mit Bryst!
Jeg fandt i ham mit Hvi - le - sted Og Trøst og Glæ - de sød,
Det Liv-sens Vand—du tør - sti - ge, Kom, drik og lev— i mig;
Min Tørst blev stil - let, og ny Kraft Ind-strøm-med' i min Sjæl;

Læg ned, du Træt - te, kom, læg ned Dit Ho - ved til mit Bryst!
Jeg fandt i ham mit Hvi - le - sted Og Trøst og Glæ - de sød.
Det Liv sens Vand—du tør - sti - ge, Kom, drik og lev— i mig."
Min Tørst blev stil - let, og ny Kraft Ind-strøm-med' i min Sjæl.

5 Igjen fornam jeg Jesu Røst:
"Det Verdens Lys er jeg:
‖:Se hen til mig, og Morg'nens Glans
Skal straale paa din Vei."‖

6 Jeg kom til Jesus, og jeg fandt
I ham min Sol saa klar,
:‖Og i dens Lys jeg vandre vil,
Til Løbet endt jeg har.:‖

79

INDEX.

REGISTER.